THROUGH
THE YEAR WITH
THE SAINTS

THROUGH
THE YEAR WITH
THE SAINTS

by
M. Basil Pennington,
O.C.S.O.

AN IMAGE BOOK
DOUBLEDAY
NEW YORK   LONDON   TORONTO   SYDNEY   AUCKLAND

AN IMAGE BOOK
Published by DOUBLEDAY, a division of
Bantam Doubleday Dell Publishing Group, Inc.,
666 Fifth Avenue, New York, New York 10103.

IMAGE, DOUBLEDAY and the portrayal of a cross
intersecting a circle are trademarks of Doubleday, a
division of Bantam Doubleday Dell Publishing Group, Inc.

Library of Congress Cataloging-in-Publication Data
Pennington, M. Basil.
Through the year with the saints.

Bibliography: p.
1. Christian saints.   I. Title.
BX4655.2.P464   1987   242'.37   87-26165
ISBN 0-385-24062-7

CONTENTS

INTRODUCTION

As we travel along through life, we tend to think of time as one thing following the other, and so we experience it. It is quite different for God. For him, all is now. Everything that ever was and ever will be is now present and alive in him. He is already, if I may so put it, enjoying the finished product: the saint that you and I will one day be. There we are with all the others saints. They are our friends, one with us in Christ, even as we are one with them in him.

Some of the saints are quite well known: Francis of Assisi, Joseph, Bernard of Clairvaux. Others are known to us personally: perhaps our own parents, relatives, and friends. Others are little known, such as Jerome Emiliani or Angela Merici. And some are known only to God and those already enjoying the heavenly communion. We find among the saints men and women, young and old and in between, mothers and fathers and children as well as life-long celibates, black and white and every shade in between, from every continent, gays and straight, rich and poor, cleric and lay, priests and religious, active and contemplative, hermits and preachers, hierarchs and servants, kings and slaves, men of war and men of peace—all of whom have found the peace of Christ.

Certainly one of the things that strikes us about the saints is the great variety found among them. Not only in themselves but in the many different paths they followed to sanctity, the many ways in which they served God and their fellows. There is no way of life that cannot be sanctified, that cannot become the path to true holiness.

The saints, all, are our friends. They care for us and hold us in their love. That is part of what being a saint means: loving the Lord our God and loving all whom he loves—everyone, loving our neighbor as ourselves. The saints walk with us; their prayers accompany us. Their example and their words can inspire and encourage us, can instruct and admonish us.

This little book invites us to begin to walk with them. You will find many friends here—some you already know and others who will be new to you. Each has a word for you. Some will particularly attract you, drawing you to themselves; their words will deeply touch you. Follow the attraction. Get to know them better. Seek out their writings and let them speak more fully to you. Because these brothers and sisters are truly alive in the Lord and present to us, we don't really just read their writings. We listen to them speak to us here and now through these their recorded words. To help you to further pursue a friendship, there is a select bibliography at the end of our short work.

As we walk through the year, not every day is occupied. The Church has always enjoyed its ferial days—empty days, when instead of concerning ourselves with a particular saint or mystery, we prefer to just rest in the essential mystery itself: the mystery of God's abiding love.

You will perhaps be surprised to find some saints not represented here. This may be because none of their words have come down to us. We have tried in each case to share some "word of life" from the particular saint himself or herself. In some instances where we do not seem to have any available, we have allowed another saint to speak for his or her friend.

We may want to use these short readings from the saints as part of our daily prayer, integrating them into the Office of Readings. Or we might prefer to sit down quietly with them at some other time in the day and commune quietly with our brother or sister in the Lord.

If walking through this book does nothing else but make us more aware that we do, by baptism, belong to a great company, that we are citizens with the saints, citizens of a kingdom that is and that is yet to come, that will be good. We are not alone on our journey. Many stand ready to walk with us and assist us in any way that we will allow them.

May we all find greater joy in knowing that we are one with the saints.

—M. Basil Pennington, O.C.S.O.
Feast of the Assumption
1987

JANUARY

JANUARY 1
Solemnity of Mary, Mother of God

The Solemnity of Mary, Mother of God, begins the year, honoring Mary as the Mother of God and placing our year and our lives wholly under her care.

If Saul, still breathing threats and murder against the disciples of the Lord to the extent of persecuting the Lord himself, became the object of such great mercy that as a result he himself was able to glory in the hope of the glory of the children of God, if he was—whether in his body or out of his body—caught up to the third heaven, there is no reason to be surprised that the holy Mother of God who had lived with her Son through all his trials from his earliest infancy, was raised bodily to heaven and exalted above the choirs of angels.

If there is joy among the angels when a single sinner repents, how can one describe the joyful, wonderful praise that goes up to God for the Virgin Mary who never sinned nor spoke a single false word? If it is true that those who were formerly darkness can become light in the Lord, shining like the sun in the kingdom of their Father, who can describe the eternal weight of the glory of the Virgin Mary, the glory of her who appeared in this world like the glowing dawn, fair as the moon, clear as the sun, of her from whom came forth the true light, enlightening every one coming into the world?

Since the Lord said, "If any one serves me, he must follow me, and where I am, there shall my servant be also," where, think you, will his Mother be, she who served him with such faithful constancy? Since she followed him and became obedient unto death, let no one be surprised at seeing her now, surpassing all the others in following the Lamb wherever he goes.

—St. Aelred of Rievaulx

JANUARY 2
St. Basil the Great and St. Gregory Nazianzen

St. Basil the Great (c. 330–379) and St. Gregory Nazianzen (329–390) were intimate friends even though they went through a period of estrangement. They pursued the monastic life, produced many treatises, especially on the Holy Spirit, and then rose to lead the Church, Basil as archbishop of Caesarea and Gregory as archbishop of Constantinople.

When in the course of time, we acknowledged our friendship and recognized our ambition was a life of true wisdom, we became everything to each other: we shared the same lodging, the same table, the same desires, the same goals. Our love for each other grew daily warmer and deeper.

—*St. Gregory*

JANUARY 4
St. Elizabeth Ann Seton

St. Elizabeth Ann Seton (1774–1821), a devoted wife and mother, converted from the Episcopal Church after her husband's death. Amid innumerable trials and suffering, she founded the Sisters of Charity and was the first native-born American to be canonized.

What was the first rule of our dear Savior's life? You know it was to do the Father's will. Well, then, the first purpose of our daily work is to do the will of God; secondly, to do it in the manner he wills; and thirdly, to do it because it is his will.

We know certainly that our God calls us to a holy life. We know that he gives us every grace, every abundant grace; and though we are so weak of ourselves, this grace is able to carry us through every obstacle and difficulty.

—*Mother Seton*

JANUARY 5
St. John Neumann

*St. John Neumann (1811–1860), an immigrant who became a Re-
demptorist and then bishop of Philadelphia, was noted for his care
for immigrants.*

When it was first announced to us that our Holy Father Pius XI had
appointed us to the pastoral care and government of this important
portion of the flock of Christ, we must confess that the heavy charge
filled our heart with anxiety. To leave those from whom we had
experienced for many years the most cordial affection; to enter upon
an entirely new sphere of duty; to assume the government of so vast
a number of souls, who would look to us to lead them on to our
heavenly home—all this urged us to implore the Lord to remove the
chalice from us. We have, however, been compelled to bow in obedience to the successor of St. Peter, knowing that whatsoever he binds
on earth shall be bound also in heaven; and submitting to the will of
God, we humbly hope that he who hath commenced in us what the
Apostle St. Paul calls "a good work" will graciously grant us that
sufficiency which is required to bring it to perfection. . . .

And now, brethren, commending you to God and to the word of
his grace, our daily prayer for you is "that your charity may more
and more abound in knowledge and in all understanding; that you
may be sincere and without offense unto the day of Christ, replen-
ished with the fruit of justice, through Jesus Christ, unto the glory
and praise of God." May our dear Mother Mary and her Son bless
you all!

—St. John

JANUARY 7
St. Raymond of Penyafort

St. Raymond of Penyafort (1175–1275), a lawyer who became a Dominican and eventually Master General of the order, was outstanding both for his canonical studies and his apostolic zeal.

Look then on Jesus, the author and preserver of faith. In complete sinlessness he suffered and at the hands of those who were his own, and was numbered among the wicked. As you drink the cup of the Lord Jesus (how glorious it is!), give thanks to the Lord, the Giver of all blessings.

May the God of love and peace set your heart at rest and speed you on your journey. May he meanwhile shelter you from disturbance by others in the hidden recesses of his love until he brings you at last into that place of complete plenitude where you will repose for ever in the vision of peace, in the security of trust and in the restful enjoyment of his riches.

—*St. Raymond*

JANUARY 12
St. Aelred of Rievaulx

St. Aelred of Rievaulx (1110–1167), the son of a priest, was raised in the court of Scotland and became a Cistercian monk at twenty-four. A friend of Saint Bernard of Clairvaux, he was elected abbot and exercised great influence in England and Scotland. He is best known for his writings on friendship.

God of mercy, hear the prayer that I offer for your people. My duty constrains me, my heart impels me, and the remembrance of your goodness compels me. Beloved Lord, you know how much I love them, how my heart is theirs and my affection, too. Lord you know that it is with neither severity nor love of power that I exercise my authority, and moreover, how greatly I long to be of service to them in charity, and that being head of them means being humble and affectionate with them as one of themselves.

So hear me, O Lord my God, hear me, and let your eyes be open day and night upon them. Spread your wings and protect them in your goodness, extend your holy power and bless them, pour your Holy Spirit into their hearts, and may he keep them in unity of spirit and in the bond of peace, chaste in body and humble of heart. May your good Spirit dwell in their thoughts so that in his light they may come to know you. May they impress on themselves the remembrance of him on whom they should call in trouble and consult in doubt. May this gentle Comforter come to the aid of all those who are grieved by temptation, and may he strengthen their weakness among the trials and difficulties of this life.

Moved by your Spirit, dear Lord, may they be at peace with one another, in themselves and with me; may they be modest and vigilant; may they be obedient; helping and bearing with one another.

May they be fervent in spirit, joyful in hope, never wearying in poverty, abstinence, toil and vigil, silence and recollection. . . . Be in the midst of them according to your solemn promise. And since you know the need of each one, I beseech you to strengthen the feeble, not to cast out the weak, to cure the sick, comfort the sorrowful, revive the weary, confirm the wavering, and may all find the help of your grace in their needs and temptations. . . .

I place them in your holy hands and commit them to your loving providence; may no one snatch them from your hand, nor from the hand of your servant to whom you have entrusted them. May they persevere joyfully in their holy resolve, and in persevering may they attain to eternal life, through your help, dear Lord, you who are living and reigning through all the ages. Amen.

—*St. Aelred*

JANUARY 13
St. Hilary of Poitiers

St. Hilary of Poitiers (d. c. 368), a married man, was converted to the faith and elected bishop of his native city around 350. An outstanding theologian, doctor of the Church, he was exiled for his opposition to the Arians.

On the Sabbath everyone without exception was commanded to do no work and to rest, remaining inactive. Why then did the Lord break the Sabbath saying: "Have you not read how on the Sabbath the priests in the Temple profane the Sabbath, and are guiltless?"

Great, indeed, are the works of God. He holds the sky in his hands and he gives light to the sun and the other planets, gives growth to the plants of the earth, maintains man in life. Yes, everything in heaven and on earth has its being and lives through the will of God the Father. Everything comes from God and everything exists through the Son. He is, in fact, the head and the principle of all things. In him everything was made. And it is out of the fullness contained in himself, according to the initiative of his eternal power that he has created everything. Now, if Christ is active in all things, it follows that it is the Father's actions which act in Christ. That is why he said: "My Father is working still and I am working." Because all that Christ does as the Son of God indwelt by God the Father is the work of the Father. Thus Christ's action goes on every day and, it seems to me, the principles of life, the formation of bodies, and the development and growth of living things manifest this action.

Then does God work on the Sabbath? He certainly does, otherwise the sky would disappear, the light of the sun would go out, the earth would fall apart, all its fountains would dry up and our life would perish if, because of the Sabbath, the moving power of the universe were to stop working. But in fact there is no cessation—during the Sabbath just as during the other six days, the elements of the universe continue to fulfill their function. For through them the Father is working now and always.

—*St. Hilary*

JANUARY 17
St. Anthony

St. Anthony (251–356), called the father of Christian monasticism, sought greater solitude for decades and then emerged to become the father of a large monastic gathering. He came out of the desert on occasion to combat heresy or succour the poor.

Let us be persuaded that we must not grow careless. We are the servants of the Lord and bound to serve him, our Master. Now, what servant would dare to say: "Since I worked yesterday, I am not working today." Nor will he count up the days he has toiled and take his rest accordingly. No, day in and day out, as it is written in the Gospel, he will show the same willingness to serve the Lord so that he may please him and not incur guilt. Let us persist in a daily practice of self-denial, knowing that if we neglect a single day in taking up our daily cross, the Lord will be displeased with us for our carelessness.

—St. Anthony

JANUARY 20
St. Fabian
and St. Sebastian

St. Fabian (d. 250), Pope since 236, and St. Sebastian (d. 300) were both martyred at Rome.

My dear brothers,

    I received your letter in which I was most fully informed of Fabian's glorious death. Through you we can see quite clearly what an example of faith and courage his death offers us. It is helpful and encouraging when a bishop offers himself as a model for his brothers and sisters by the constancy of his faith.

                                  —*St. Cyprian*

JANUARY 21
St. Agnes

St. Agnes (d. c. 304), noble and beautiful, consecrated her virginity to Christ and was beheaded in witness to him.

Today is the birthday of a virgin, let us imitate her purity. It is the birthday of a martyr, let us offer ourselves in sacrifice. It is the birthday of Saint Agnes, who is said to have suffered martyrdom at the age of twelve.

There was little or no room in that small body for a wound. Yet she shows no fear of the blood-stained hands of her executioners. She offers her whole body to be put to the sword by fierce soldiers. She is too young to know death, yet is ready to face it. Dragged against her will to the pagan altars, she stretches out her hands to the Lord in the midst of the flames, making the triumphant sign of Christ the victor on the altars of sacrilege. She puts her neck and hands in iron chains, but no chain can hold fast her tiny limbs. In the midst of tears she sheds not tears for herself. She stood still, she prayed, she offered her neck. You could see fear in the eyes of her executioner, as if he was the one condemned. His right hand trembled, his face grew pale as he saw the girl's peril, while she had no fear for herself. One victim, but a twin martyrdom, to modesty and religion, Agnes preserved her virginity and gained a martyr's crown.

—St. Ambrose

JANUARY 22
St. Vincent

St. Vincent (d. 304), a permanent deacon of the diocese of Saragossa in Spain, suffered terrible torture and death rather than deny Christ and hand over the Sacred Scriptures to be profaned.

"To you has been granted in Christ's behalf not only that you should believe in him but also that you should suffer for him."

Vincent had received both these gifts and held them as his own. For how could he have them if he had not received them? He displayed his faith in what he said, his endurance in what he suffered.

No one ought to be confident in his own strength when he undergoes temptation. For when ever we endure evils courageously, our long-suffering comes from Christ.

He once said to his disciples, "In this world you will suffer persecution," and then, to allay their fears, he added, "But rest assured, I have conquered the world."

There is no need to wonder then, my dearly beloved brothers and sisters, that Vincent conquered in him who conquered the world. It offers temptation to lead us astray; it strikes terror into us to break our spirit. Hence if our personal pleasures do not hold us captive, and if we are not frightened by brutality, then the world is overcome. At both of these approaches Christ rushes to our aid and the Christian is not conquered.

—St. Augustine

JANUARY 24
St. Francis de Sales

St. Francis de Sales (1567–1622), noble, brilliant, zealous, gentle, the bishop of Geneva, brought many Calvinists back to the Church. Co-founder of the Visitation Nuns and author of spiritual classics, he was beatified the year he died, later canonized and declared a Doctor of the Church and patron of writers and of the press.

My intention is to instruct those living in towns, in households, whose circumstances oblige them outwardly to live an ordinary life; and who, very often, are not willing even to think of undertaking the devout life, saying it is impossible. Their idea is that no one living in the pressure of the world should aspire to Christian piety.

I will show them that a determined person can live in the world untainted. It is not easy! I should like many to undertake it with more zeal than before.

Weak though I am, I hope to contribute some little of my own to those who undertake this enterprise with a generous heart.

True living devotion presupposes the love of God, indeed, it is itself a true love of him in the highest form. Divine love, enlightening our soul and making us pleasing to God, is called grace. Giving us power to do good, it is called charity. When it reaches the point of perfection where it makes us earnestly, frequently and readily do good, it is called devotion.

—St. Francis

JANUARY 25
Conversion of
St. Paul, Apostle

Jesus came upon St. Paul when he was on his way to Damascus to persecute those who followed "the Way." Paul was open to the experience, welcomed the faith, received baptism, and became an apostle.

From Paul to the churches of Galatia, and from all the brothers who are here with me, an apostle who does not owe his authority to men or his appointment to any human being but who has been appointed by Jesus Christ and by God the Father who raised Jesus from the dead. . . .

The fact is, brothers and sisters, and I want you to realize this, the Good News I preached is not a human message that I was given by men, it is something I learnt only through a revelation of Jesus Christ. You must have heard of my career as a practicing Jew, how merciless I was in persecuting the Church of God, how much damage I did to it, how I stood out among other Jews of my generation, and how enthusiastically I was for the traditions of my ancestors.

Then God, who had specially chosen me while I was still in my mother's womb, called me through his grace and chose to reveal his Son to me, so that I might preach the Good News about him to the pagans. I did not stop to discuss this with any human being, nor did I go up to Jerusalem to see those who were already apostles before me, but I went off to Arabia at once and later went straight back from there to Damascus. Even when after three years I went to Jerusalem to visit Cephas and stayed with him for fifteen days, I did not see any of the other apostles; I only saw James, the brother of the

Lord, and I swear before God that what I have just written is the literal truth. After that I went to Syria and Cilicia, and was still not known by sight to the churches of Christ in Judea, who had heard nothing except that their one-time persecutor was now preaching the faith he had previously tried to destroy; and they gave glory to God for me.

—St. Paul

JANUARY 26
St. Timothy and St. Titus

St. Timothy and St. Titus were disciples of St. Paul. Timothy became shepherd of the church at Ephesus and Titus of that in Crete.

From Paul a servant of God, an apostle of Jesus Christ . . . to Titus, true child of mine in the faith that we share, wishing you grace and peace from God the Father and from Christ Jesus our Savior.

The reason I left you behind in Crete was for you to get everything organized there and appoint elders in every town, in the way I told you. . . .

It is for you, then, to preach the behavior which goes with healthy doctrine. The older men should be reserved, dignified, moderate, sound in faith and love and constancy. Similarly, the older women should behave as though they were religious, with no scandalmongering, and no habitual wine-drinking—they are to be the teachers of right behavior and show the younger women how they should love their husbands and love their children, how they are to be sensible and chaste, and how to work in their homes, and be gentle, and do as their husbands tell them, so that the message of God is never disgraced. In the same way, you have got to persuade the younger men to be moderate, and in everything you do make yourself an example to them of working for good: when you are teaching, be an example to them in your sincerity and earnestness and in keeping all that you say so wholesome that nobody can make objections to it, and then any opponent will be at a loss, with no accusations to make against us.

—St. Paul

JANUARY 27
St. Angela Merici

St. Angela Merici (1470–1535), a member of the Third Order of St. Francis, when she was fifty-seven founded the Company of St. Ursula (to become forty years later a religious congregation, the Ursulines to instruct poor girls in the Christian faith).

As our Savior says, "A good tree is not able to produce bad fruit." He says, a good tree, that is, a good heart as well as a soul on fire with charity can do nothing but good and holy works. For this reason Saint Augustine said, "Love, and do what you will." Namely, possess love and charity and then do what you will.

Mothers of children, even if they have a thousand, carry each and every one fixed in their hearts, and because of the strength of their love they do not forget any of them. In fact, it seems that the more children they have the more their love and care for each one is increased.

Be sincerely kind to every one according to the words of our Lord, "Learn of me, for I am meek and humble of heart." Thus you are imitating God, of whom it is said, "He has disposed all things pleasantly." And again Jesus said, "My yoke is easy and my burden light."

—St. Angela

JANUARY 28
St. Thomas Aquinas

St. Thomas Aquinas (1225–1274), one of the greatest theologians in the history of the Church, entered the Dominicans when he was nineteen. He taught for many years at the University of Paris and wrote a summation of theology which became basic in theological education.

Jesus said: "I am the good shepherd." The title of shepherd manifestly belongs to Christ. For just as a shepherd takes his flock out to pasture, so does Christ refresh the faithful with spiritual food, his own Body and his own Blood.

The title of shepherd he has given to others, to certain members of his Body. Peter was a shepherd, and the other apostles, and all the bishops. "I will give you shepherds," he said through Jeremiah, "shepherds after my own heart." Although the leaders of the Church —his sons—are all shepherds, Christ said, "I am the good shepherd," to indicate the unique power of his own love. No other shepherd is good unless he is united to Christ by love, thus becoming a living member of the true shepherd.

The work of the good shepherd is love. That is why Jesus said that he would lay down his life for his sheep. The salvation of the spiritual flock matters more than the shepherd's life. That is why when the flock is in danger, its shepherd must be ready to lay down his physical life for his sheep.

—*St. Thomas Aquinas*

JANUARY 31
St. John Bosco

St. John Bosco (1815–1888), founder of the Salesians, later called the Society of Don Bosco, devoted his life primarily to the care of boys and young men. He also founded the Daughters of Our Lady, Help of Christians to care for poor and neglected girls.

If you wish to show your sympathy with the real good of our pupils, and to get them to do their duty, it is most important never to forget that you represent the parents of these beloved young people who have always been the tender object of my preoccupations and studies, of my priestly ministry and of our Salesian Society.

If, therefore, you are real fathers to your pupils, you must also have a father's heart. How many times, my beloved sons, in my long career, I have had to acknowledge the following great truth: it is undoubtedly easier to lose one's temper than to exercise patience, to threaten rather than persuade a child. I must say too, it suits our impatience and our pride better to punish those who resist us rather than to correct them, bearing with them firmly and kindly. The love I recommend to you is that with which Saint Paul treated the faithful newly converted to belief in the Lord. Often they called forth his tears and entreaties when he saw them less amenable and less inclined to response to his zeal.

As they are our children, let us avoid all anger when we have to check their faults, or at least let us moderate it so as to seem calm. No emotional agitations, no scornful glances, nor insulting speeches. Let us feel rather compassion in the present, and hope for the future. You will then be real fathers and your correction will be effective. Let us think of those over whom we have to exercise our authority as your children. Let us put ourselves as it were at their service, like

Jesus who came to obey and not to command. Remember that education must come from the heart and that God alone is the master. We cannot but fail if God does not teach us the art and give us the keys to it.

—St. John

FEBRUARY

FEBRUARY 2
Presentation of the Lord

When our Lord was forty days old, Joseph and Mary brought him to the Temple to fulfill the requirement of the Law in regard to a first-born son.

In honor of the divine mystery that we celebrate today, let us hasten to meet Christ. Everyone should be eager to join in the procession and to carry a light.

Our lighted candles are a sign of the divine splendor of the one who comes to expel the dark shadow of evil and to make the whole universe radiant with the brilliance of his eternal light. Our candles also show how bright our souls should be when we go to meet Christ.

The Mother of God, the most pure Virgin, carried the true light in her arms and brought him to those who lay in darkness. We too should carry a light for all to see and reflect the radiance of the true light as we hasten to meet him.

The light has come and has shone upon a world enveloped in shadows, the Dayspring from on high has visited us and given light to those who live in darkness. This, then, is our feast, and we join in procession with lighted candles to reveal the light that has shone upon us and the glory that is yet to come to us through him. So let us hasten all together to meet our God.

The true light has come, "the light that enlightens every one who is born into this world." Let all of us, my brothers and sisters, be enlightened and made radiant by this light. Let all of us share in its splendor, and be so filled with it that no one remains in the darkness.

—St. Sophronius

FEBRUARY 5
St. Agatha

St. Agatha, a popular virgin martyr, according to the tradition, suffered martyrdom in Sicily because of her fidelity to Christ and to her virginity.

Agatha, the name of our saint, means "good." She was truly good, for she lived as a child of God. She was also given as the gift of God, the source of all goodness to her bridegroom, Christ, and to us. For she grants us a share in her goodness.

This woman who invites us to her celebration is both a wife and virgin. To use the analogy of Paul, she is the bride who has been betrothed to one husband, Christ. A true virgin, she wore the glow of a pure conscience and the crimson of the Lamb's blood for her cosmetics. Again and again she meditated on the death of her eager lover. For her, Christ's death was recent, his blood was still moist. Her robe is the mark of her faithful witness to Christ. It bears the indelible marks of his crimson blood and the shining threads of her eloquence. She offers to all who come after her these treasures of her eloquent confession.

—*St. Methodius of Sicily*

FEBRUARY 8
St. Jerome Emiliani

St. Jerome (1486–1537) underwent a conversion while he was a prisoner of war. Escaping, he returned to Venice to care for the sick and poor. Later he became a priest and founded the Society of the Servants of the Poor or the Clerks Regular of Somaschi.

I urge you to persevere in your love for Christ and your faithful observance of the law of Christ.

Our goal is God, the source of all good. As we say in our prayer, we are to place our trust in God and in no one else. In his kindness, our Lord wished to strengthen your faith, for without it, as the evangelist points out, Christ could not have performed many of his miracles. He also wished to listen to your prayer and so he ordained that you experience poverty, distress, abandonment, weariness and scorn.

God alone knows the reason for all of this, yet we can recognize three causes. In the first place, our blessed Lord is telling you that he desires to include you among his beloved sons, provided that you remain steadfast in his ways, for this is the way he treats his friends and makes them holy.

The second reason is that he is asking you to grow continually in your confidence in him alone and not in others.

Now there is a third reason. God wishes to test you like gold in the furnace. The dross is consumed by the fire, but the pure gold remains and its value increases. It is in this manner that God acts with his good servant who puts his hope in him and remains unshaken in times of distress. God raises him up and, in return for the things he has left out of love for God, he repays him hundredfold in this life and with eternal life hereafter.

If then you remain constant in faith in the face of trial, the Lord will give you peace and rest for a time in this world and for ever in the next.

—*St. Jerome*

FEBRUARY 10
St. Scholastica

St. Scholastica (d. 543), sister of St. Benedict of Nursia, founded a monastery of nuns at Plombariola under the guidance of her brother.

Scholastica, the sister of blessed Benedict, who had been consecrated to almighty God from early childhood, used to visit her brother once a year. On these occasions the man of God would go down to meet her in a house belonging to the monastery, a short distance from the entrance.

One day her brother met her there according to their custom with a few of his disciples, and they spent the entire day singing God's praises and conversing about the spiritual life. When darkness was setting in, they took their meal together.

Since they continued their conversation until it was quite late, the holy nun said to him, "Please do not leave me tonight; let us keep talking about the joys of heaven until morning." "What are you saying, sister?" he replied. "You know I cannot stay away from the monastery."

Then that holy nun folded her hands on the table and rested her head on them in earnest prayer to the almighty Lord. When she looked up again, there was a sudden burst of lightning and thunder, accompanied by such a downpour that neither Benedict nor his companions could set foot outside the door.

Then the man of God began to complain bitterly, "God forgive you, sister; what have you done?" She answered, "I appealed to you and you would not listen to me. So I turned to my God and he heard my prayer. Leave now if you can. Leave me and return to your monastery."

And he, who had not wanted to remain there of his own will, had no choice but to stay in spite of his unwillingness. Thus, they passed the whole night together and both derived great profit from the holy thoughts they exchanged about the spiritual life.

We need not be surprised that in this instance the woman proved to be mightier than her brother. For, since, according to John "God is love," it is no more than right that her influence should be greater than his, for her love was greater.

—*St. Gregory the Great*

FEBRUARY 11
Our Lady of Lourdes

In 1858 the blessed Virgin Mary appeared eighteen times to Berna-
dette at Massabielle, Lourdes, where she indicated a spring, whose
waters have been used to perform numerous miracles.

I am the Immaculate Conception.

—*Blessed Virgin Mary*

FEBRUARY 14
St. Cyril and St. Methodius

St. Cyril (c. 827–869) and St. Methodius (c. 826–884), brothers from Greece, monks, Apostles to the Slavs, invented an alphabet that marked the beginning of Slavonic literature and liturgy.

I began to praise the Creator as I saw the earth firmly stable, and living creatures in such variety and the blossoms of plants with their many hues. It is the nature of things which come into existence to derive their origin from what is already existing. And it seemed to me that it might be said with equal truth that nothing is eternally co-existent with God distinct from himself but that whatever exists has its origin from him. I was persuaded of this also by the undeniable dispositions of the elements and by the orderly arrangement of nature about them.

—St. Methodius

FEBRUARY 21
St. Peter Damian

*St. Peter Damian, a brilliant teacher at Ravenna, at eighteen be-
came a hermit at Fonte Avellana. For five years he reluctantly served
the Church as a cardinal legate before he was allowed to resume his
eremitical life.*

Epitaph
on the tomb of St. Peter Damian
written by himself:

What you are, I was;
what I am, you will be.
Remember me, I pray you.
Have pity on the dust of Peter
who lies here.

FEBRUARY 22
Feast of the
Chair of St. Peter

St. Peter the Apostle came to lead the Church at Rome, establishing his "chair" there, where he eventually suffered martyrdom.

Out of the whole world one man, Peter, is chosen to preside at the calling of all the nations and to be set over all the apostles and all the fathers of the Church. Though there are among God's people many bishops and many shepherds, Peter is thus appointed to rule in his own person those whom Christ also rules as the original ruler. Beloved, how great and wonderful is this sharing in his power that God in his goodness has given to this man. Whatever Christ has willed to be shared in common by Peter and the other leaders of the Church, it is only through Peter that he has given to others what he has not refused to bestow on them.

Jesus said, "Upon this rock I will build my Church, and the gates of hell shall not prevail against it." On this strong foundation, he says, I will build an everlasting temple. The great height of my Church, which is to penetrate the heavens, shall rise on the firm foundation of this faith.

Blessed Peter is therefore told, "To you I will give the keys of the kingdom of heaven. Whatever you bind on earth shall be bound also in heaven. Whatever you loose on earth shall be loosed also in heaven."

—St. Leo the Great

FEBRUARY 23
St. Polycarp

St. Polycarp (c. 69–c. 158), a disciple of St. John the Beloved Disciple, became the bishop of Smyrna. He suffered martyrdom in his old age.

Be steadfast and follow the Lord's example, strong and unshaken in faith, loving the community as you love one another. United in truth, show the Lord's own gentleness in your dealings with one another, and look down on no one. If you can do good, do not put it off, because almsgiving frees one from death.

—*St. Polycarp*

MARCH

MARCH 8
St. John of God

St. John of God (1495–1550), after his military service, devoted himself to the care of the sick. He founded in Granada, Spain, the Order of Hospitallers.

So many poor people come here that I very often wonder how we can care for them all, but Jesus Christ provides all things and nourishes everyone. Many of them come to the House of God, because the city of Granada is large and very cold, especially now in winter. More than a hundred and ten are now living here, sick and healthy, servants and pilgrims. Since this house is open to everyone, it receives the sick of every type and condition: the crippled, the disabled, lepers, mutes, the insane, paralytics, those suffering from scurvy and those bearing the affliction of old age, many children, and above all countless pilgrims and travelers, who come here and for whom we furnish the fire, water and salt, as well as the utensils to cook their food. And for all of this no payment is requested, yet Christ provides.

I work here on borrowed money, a prisoner for the sake of Jesus Christ. And often my debts are so pressing that I dare not go out of the house for fear of being seized by my creditors. Whenever I see so many poor brothers and neighbors of mine suffering beyond their strength and overwhelmed with so many physical or mental ills which I cannot alleviate, then I become exceedingly sorrowful but I trust in Christ, who knows my heart. And so I say, "Woe to the one who trusts in men rather than in Christ."

—*St. John*

MARCH 9
St. Gregory of Nyssa

*St. Gregory of Nyssa (c. 330–c. 395), bishop of Nyssa, brother of
Saint Basil, suffered much persecution and exile. He left us many
theological works and commentaries on Sacred Scripture.*

Paul teaches the power of Christ's name when he calls him the power
and wisdom of God, our peace, the unapproachable light, where God
dwells, our expiation and redemption, our great High Priest, our
Paschal sacrifice, our propitiation; when he declares him to be the
radiance of God's glory, the very pattern of his nature, the creator of
all ages, our spiritual food and drink, the cornerstone, the visible
image of the invisible God.

He goes on to speak of him as the mighty God, the Head of his
Body the Church, the first born of the new creation, and the Media-
tor between God and us, the only-begotten Son crowned with glory
and honor.

—St. Gregory

MARCH 17
St. Patrick

St. Patrick (c. 389–c. 461), the Apostle of Ireland, after years of study and spiritual preparation at the monastery of Lerins, brought the Irish people to the Catholic faith.

I rise today
Through a mighty strength, the invocation of the Trinity,
Through belief in the threeness,
Through confession of the oneness
Of the Creator of Creation.

I rise today
Through the strength of Christ's birth with his baptism,
Through the strength of his crucifixion with his burial,
Through the strength of his resurrection with his ascension,
Through the strength of his descent for the judgment of doom.

I rise today
Through the strength of the love of Cherubim,
In the obedience of the angels,
In the service of the archangels,

In hope of resurrection to meet with reward,
In prayers of patriarchs,
In predictions of prophets,
In preachings of apostles,
In faiths of confessors,
In innocence of holy virgins,
In deeds of righteous men.

I rise today
through the strength of heaven;
Light of sun,
Radiance of moon,
Splendor of fire,
Speed of lightning
Swiftness of wind,
Depths of sea,
Stability of earth,
Firmness of rock.

I rise today
Through God's strength to pilot me,
God's might to uphold me,
God's wisdom to guide me,
God's eye to look before me,
God's ear to hear me,
God's word to speak for me,
God's hand to guard me,
God's way to lie before me,
God's shield to protect me,
God's host to save me
From snares of devils,
From temptation of vices,
From every one who shall wish me ill,
Afar and near,
alone and in a multitude.

Christ to shield me today
Against poison, against burning,
Against drowning, against wounding,
So that there may come to me abundance of reward.
Christ with me, Christ before me, Christ behind me,
Christ in me, Christ beneath me, Christ above me,
Christ on my right, Christ on my left,
Christ when I lie down, Christ when I sit down,
   Christ when I arise,
Christ in the heart of everyone who thinks of me,
Christ in the mouth of everyone who speaks of me,

Christ in every eye that sees me,
Christ in every ear that hears me.

I rise today
Through a mighty strength, the invocation of the Trinity,
Through belief in the threeness,
Through confession of the oneness
Of the Creator of Creation.

—*St. Patrick*

MARCH 18
St. Cyril of Jerusalem

*St. Cyril of Jerusalem (315–386), bishop of Jerusalem, suffered re-
peated exile at the hands of the Arians but remained steadfast in his
faith till the end.*

The Lord Jesus on the night when he was betrayed, took bread and
when he had given thanks, he broke it and said, "Take this and eat,
this is my body." Then taking the cup he said, "Take this and drink;
this is my blood." Since, then, he himself has declared and said of the
bread, "This is my body," who shall dare to doubt it any longer?
And since he has affirmed and said, "This is my blood," who shall
ever hesitate, saying that this is not his blood?

Therefore with fullest assurance let us partake as of the body and
blood of Christ, for in the figure of bread his body is given to you and
in the figure of wine, his blood; so that by partaking of the body and
blood of Christ you might be made the same body and blood with
him. So do we come to bear Christ in us, because his body and blood
are diffused through our members, so it is that, according to blessed
Peter, "we become partakers of the divine nature."

Christ when discoursing with the Jews once said, "Unless you eat the flesh of the Son of Man and drink his blood, you have no life in you." They, by not receiving his saying spiritually were offended, and left him, thinking that he was inviting them to eat flesh.

Even under the Old Testament, there was shewbread; but since it belonged to the Old Testament, this came to an end; but in the New Testament there is the bread of heaven and the cup of salvation, sanctifying soul and body; for as the bread has respect to our body so then is the Word appropriate to our soul.

Contemplate therefore bread and wine not as bare elements for they are, according to the Lord's declaration, the body and blood of Christ.

—St. Cyril

MARCH 19
St. Joseph

St. Joseph, the husband of the Blessed Virgin Mary, served as the father of Jesus Christ during Jesus' early formative years on earth.

There is a general rule concerning all special graces granted to any human being. Whenever the divine favor chooses someone to receive a special grace, or to accept a lofty vocation, God adorns the person chosen with all the gifts of the Spirit needed to fulfill the task at hand.

This general rule is especially verified in the case of St. Joseph, the foster-father of our Lord and the husband of the Queen of our world, enthroned above the angels. He was chosen by the eternal Father as the trustworthy guardian and protector of his greatest treasures, namely, his divine Son and Mary, Joseph's wife. He carried out this vocation with complete fidelity until at last God called him, saying, "Good and faithful servant, enter into the joy of your Lord."

Remember us, St. Joseph, and plead for us to your foster-child.

Ask your most holy bride, the Virgin Mary, to look kindly upon us, since she is the mother of him who with the Father and the Holy Spirit lives and reigns eternally.

—St. Bernardine of Siena

MARCH 20
St. Cuthbert

St. Cuthbert (d. 687), a poor shepherd as a boy, became in time the shepherd of several monasteries and then, after a period of eremitical life, shepherd of the diocese of Lindesfarne.

Now when his dwelling place and chambers had been built with the help of his brethren, Cuthbert, the man of God, began to dwell alone. At first, indeed, he used to go forth from his cell to meet the brethren who came to him and to minister to them. And when he had devoutly washed their feet in warm water, he was sometimes compelled by them to take off his shoes and to allow them to wash his feet. For he had so far withdrawn his mind from the care of his body and fixed it on the care of his soul alone that having once been shod with the boots of skin that he was accustomed to use, he would wear them for whole months together. And let it be said that once he had put his boots on at Easter, he did not take them off until Easter came round again a year later, and then only for the washing of the feet which takes place on Maundy Thursday. On account of the frequent genuflections he made at prayer while wearing his boots, he was found to have a long thick callus at the junction of his feet and his shins.

Then, when his zeal for perfection grew, he shut himself up in the hermitage, and, remote from the gaze of all, he learned to live a solitary life of fasting, prayers and vigils, rarely having conversation from within his cell with visitors and that only through a window. At first he opened this and rejoiced to see and be seen by the brethren with whom he spoke. But as time went on, he shut even that and opened it only for the sake of giving his blessing or for some other definite necessity.

—*St. Bede the Venerable*

MARCH 21
St. Benedict

St. Benedict (c. 480–c. 547), after years of lived experience and founding monasteries at Subiaco and Monte Casino, wrote a monastic rule that became normative for most monks and nuns in the West. He was declared patron protector of Europe.

An abbot who is worthy to rule a monastery should always remember what he is called, and realize in his actions the name of superior. For he is believed to be the representative of Christ in the monastery, and for that reason is called by a name of the Lord, according to the words of the Apostle, "You have received the spirit of adoption of sons, whereby we cry, Abba, Father." Let him realize how difficult and arduous a task he has undertaken of ruling souls and adapting himself to many dispositions. One he must humor, another rebuke, another persuade, according to each one's dispositions and understanding, and thus adapt and accommodate himself to all in such a way that he may not only suffer no loss in the sheep committed to him, but may even rejoice in the increase of a good flock.

Let the abbot consider always what an office he has undertaken and to whom he must render an account of his stewardship, and let him know that it is his duty rather to profit his brethren than to preside over them. Let him always set mercy above judgment so that he himself may obtain mercy. Let him hate ill-doing but love the brethren. In administering correction, let him act with prudent moderation, lest being too zealous in removing the rust he break the vessel. Let him always distrust his own frailty and remember that the bruised reed is not to be broken. By this we do not mean that he should allow evils to grow but that as we have said above, he should eradicate them prudently and with charity, in the way which may seem best in each case. And let him study rather to be loved than feared. Let him not be turbulent nor anxious, overbearing nor obstinate, jealous nor too suspicious, for otherwise he will never be at rest. Let him be prudent and considerate in all his commands and whether the work which he enjoins concerns God or the world, let him always be discreet and moderate. Let him so temper all things that the strong may still want to do more and the weak not draw back in alarm. And especially, let him keep this present rule in all things, so that having ministered faithfully he may hear from the Lord what the good servant heard who gave his fellow servants wheat in due season: "Amen, I say to you, he will set him over all his goods."

—St. Benedict

MARCH 25
The Feast of
the Annunciation

The angel Gabriel was sent from God to inform Mary of God's designs and receive her assent to becoming the Mother of God.

Virgin, you have heard what will happen, you have heard how it will happen. You have a double reason for astonishment and rejoicing. Rejoice, O Daughter of Sion, and be exceeding glad, Daughter of Jerusalem. And since you have heard joyous and glad tidings, let us hear that joyous reply we long for, so that broken bones may rejoice.

You have heard what is to happen, I say, and you have believed. Believe also the way you have heard it is to happen. You have heard that you will conceive and bear a son; you have heard that it will be by the Holy Spirit and not by a man. The angel is waiting for your reply. It is time for him to return to the one who sent him. We, too, are waiting for this merciful word, my Lady, we who are miserably weighed down under a sentence of condemnation. The price of our salvation is being offered you. If you consent, we shall immediately be set free. We all have been made in the eternal Word of God, and look, we are dying. In your brief reply we can all be restored and so brought back to life. Doleful Adam and his unhappy offspring, exiled from Paradise, implores you, kind Virgin, to give this answer; David asks it, Abraham asks it, all the other holy patriarchs, your very own fathers beg it of you, as do those now dwelling in the region of the shadow of death. For it the whole world is waiting, bowed down at your feet. And rightly so, because on your answer depends the comfort of the afflicted, the redemption of captives, the deliverance of the damned, the salvation of all the sons and daughters of Adam, your whole race. Give your answer quickly, my Virgin. My Lady, say this word which earth and hell and heaven itself are waiting for. The very King and Lord of all, he who has so desired your beauty, is waiting anxiously for your answer and assent, by which he proposes to save the world.

"Behold," she says, "I am the handmaiden of the Lord; let it be done to me according to your word."

—*St. Bernard of Clairvaux*

APRIL

APRIL 2
St. Francis of Paolo

St. Francis of Paolo (1416–1507), who became a hermit at the age of thirteen, founded the hermits of St. Francis of Assisi or the Order of Minims. Later he entered upon a more active apostolate and spent his last years serving in the court of the King of France.

Fix your minds on the passion of our Lord Jesus Christ. Inflamed with love for us, he came down from heaven to redeem us. For our sake he endured every torment of body and soul and shrank from no bodily pain. He himself gave us an example of perfect patience and love. We, then, are to be patient in adversity.

Take pains to refrain from sharp words. Pardon one another so that later on you will not remember the injury. The recollection of an injury is itself wrong. It adds to our anger, nurtures our sin and hates what is good. It is a rusty arrow and poison for the soul. It puts all virtue to flight.

Be peace-loving. Peace is a precious treasure to be sought with great zeal. You are well aware that our sins arouse God's anger. You must change your life, so that God in his mercy will pardon you. What we conceal from each other is known to God. Be converted, then, with a sincere heart. Live your life that you may receive the blessings of the Lord. Then the peace of God our Father will be with you always.

—*St. Francis*

APRIL 4
St. Isidore of Seville

*St. Isidore of Seville (c. 560–636), a Doctor of the Church, was a
leader in the early development of the Church in Spain. He also
developed the Mazarabic liturgy.*

Prayer purifies us, reading instructs us. Both are good when both are
possible. Otherwise, prayer is better than reading.

If one wants to be always in God's company, he must pray regularly and read regularly. When we pray, we talk to God; when we
read, God talks to us.

Reading Holy Scripture confers two benefits. It trains the mind to
understand them; it turns our attention from the follies of the world
and leads us to the love of God.

The conscientious reader will be more concerned to carry out what
he has read than merely to acquire knowledge of it. In reading we
aim at knowing, but we must put into practice what we have learned
in our course of study.

One who is slow to grasp things but who really tries hard is rewarded; equally he who does not cultivate his God-given intellectual
ability is condemned for despising his gifts and sinning by sloth.

—St. Isidore

APRIL 5
St. Vincent Ferrer

St. Vincent Ferrer (1350–1419), who entered the Dominicans when he was seventeen, was one of the most powerful preachers of his time. He supported the antipopes, Clement VII and Benedict XIII, but when he perceived his error, he worked effectively for the healing of the schism.

If you truly want to help the soul of your neighbor, you should approach God first with all your heart. Ask him simply to fill you with charity, the greatest of all virtues; with it you can accomplish what you desire.

—*St. Vincent*

APRIL 7
St. John Baptist de la Salle

St. John Baptist de la Salle (1651–1719), a wealthy young priest, got involved, almost against his will, with the education of poor boys and founded the Brothers of Christian Schools to carry on his work.

Be driven by the love of God, because Jesus Christ died for all, that those who live may live not for themselves but for him who died and rose for them.

—*St. John*

APRIL 13
St. Martin

St. Martin (d. 659), who was elected Pope in 649, suffered much at the hands of the emperor and died in exile. He is considered a martyr.

Indeed, I have been amazed and continue to be amazed at the lack of perception and callousness of those who were once connected with me, both my friends and my relatives. They have all completely forgotten about my unhappy state, and do not care to know where I am, whether I am alive or dead.

But "God wishes all men to be saved and to come to knowledge of the truth" through the prayers of Peter. Hence I pray that God will strengthen their hearts in the orthodox faith, help them to stand firm against every heretic and enemy of the Church, and guard them unshaken. In this way, together with me in humiliation, they will receive the crown of justice in the true faith from the hand of our Lord and Savior Jesus Christ. For the Lord himself will take care of this lowly body of mine as befits his providence, whether this means unending sufferings or some small consolation. Why am I anxious? "The Lord is near." But my hope is in his compassion that he will not delay in putting an end to this course which he has assigned to me.

—*St. Martin*

APRIL 21
St. Anselm

St. Anselm (1033–1109), abbot of Bec, a great theologian and Doctor of the Church, was elected archbishop of Canterbury in 1092. He suffered a great deal for his steadfast defense of the rights of the Church.

And now, my Lord God, reveal to my heart where and how to seek you, where and how to find you. If, Lord, you are not here, if you are absent, where shall I look for you; and if you are present everywhere, why can I not see you? It is true, I know, that you dwell in inaccessible light. But where is the inaccessible light, and how shall I attain to this inaccessible light? Who will lead me to it and plunge me into it that I may see you there? Lord God, I have never seen you, I do not know your face. What, most hidden Lord, can this exile far from you do? What can your servant do who longs for your love and is cast out far from your face? He longs to see you, and your face is utterly hidden from him. His desire is to be with you, and your dwelling place is beyond reach. He wants to find you, and does not know where you are. He has set himself to seek you, and he does not know what you look like. Lord, you are my God, you are my master, and I have never seen you. You have created and recreated me. You have supported me with all I possess and I do not yet know you. You made me, in order that I might see you and I have not yet realized my destiny.

—St. Anselm

APRIL 23
St. George

St. George (fourth century), a soldier-martyr, became an almost legendary character. He is honored as the national patron of many nations and of soldiers.

St. George was a man who abandoned one army for another. He gave up the rank of tribune to enlist as a soldier for Christ. Eager to encounter the enemy, he first stripped away his worldly wealth by giving all he had to the poor. Then, freed and unencumbered, bearing the shield of faith, he plunged into the thick of the battle, an ardent soldier for Christ.

Clearly what he did serves to teach us a valuable lesson: if we are afraid to strip ourselves of our worldly possessions, then we are unfit to make a strong defense of the faith.

Let us not only admire the courage of this fighter in heaven's army but follow his example. Let us be inspired to strive for the reward of heavenly glory. We must now cleanse ourselves, as St. Paul tells us, from all defilement of body and spirit, so that one day we too may deserve to enter that temple of blessedness to which we now aspire.

—*St. Peter Damian*

APRIL 25
St. Mark

St. Mark, a relative of St. Barnabas, traveled with him and St. Paul. Later he was with St. Peter in Rome and wrote a Gospel based upon all he learned from him. He is traditionally considered the founder of the Church in Alexandria.

Judas, one of the Twelve, came up with a number of men armed with swords and clubs, sent by the chief priests and the scribes and the elders. Now the traitor had arranged a signal with them, "The one I kiss," he had said, "he is the man. Take him in charge, and see he is well guarded when you lead him away." So when the traitor came, he went straight up to Jesus and said, "Rabbi!" and kissed him. The others seized him and took him in charge. Then one of the bystanders drew his sword and struck out at the high priest's servant, and cut off his ear.

Then Jesus spoke, "Am I a brigand," he said, "that you had to come out to capture me with swords and clubs? I was among you teaching in the Temple day after day and you never laid hands on me. But this is to fulfill the Scriptures." And they all deserted him and ran away. A young man who followed him had nothing on but a linencloth. They caught hold of him, but he left the cloth in their hands and ran away naked.

—St. Mark

APRIL 28
St. Louis
Grignon de Montford

By the intensity of his piety and zeal St. Louis Grignon de Montford (1673–1716), author of the True Devotion to the Blessed Virgin Mary, *constantly evoked opposition yet he succeeded in founding two religious congregations which continue to flourish, the Daughters of Wisdom and the Missionaries of the Company of Mary.*

Hail Mary, Daughter of God the Father! Hail Mary, Mother of God the Son! Hail Mary, Spouse of the Holy Spirit! Hail Mary, Temple of the Most Holy Trinity!

Place yourself, O faithful Virgin, as a seal on my heart, that in you and through you I may be found faithful to God. Grant, most gracious Virgin, that I may be numbered among those whom you are pleased to love, to teach, and to guide, to favor, and to protect as your children.

—*St. Louis*

APRIL 29
St. Odo of Cluny

St. Odo of Cluny (c. 879–942), well-educated and of noble back-
ground, joined St. Berno in founding Cluny and succeeded him as
abbot.

Son of the Highest, deign to cast
On us a pitying eye,
You who repentant Magdalen
Called to endless joy.

O Jesus, balm of every wound!
The sinners' only stay!
Wash in Magdalen's pure tears
Our guilty spots away.

—*St. Odo*

APRIL 30
St. Catherine of Siena

St. Catherine of Siena (1347–1380), a great mystic, became a Dominican tertiary at the age of sixteen and devoted herself to the care of the poor and sick. She was led by the Lord to intervene in great affairs of Church and State and succeeded in bringing the papacy back to Rome after a long exile in France.

I know of no means of savoring the truth and living with it, without self-knowledge. It is this knowledge that makes us really understand that we are nothing, and that our being came from God when we were created in his likeness and image. And also that God created us a second time in giving us the life of grace through the blood of his only Son, blood which has shown us the truth of God the Father.

This is the divine truth: God has created us for the glory and praise of his name, to enable us to participate in his eternal beauty and to sanctify us in him. And the proof that this is the truth? The blood of the spotless Lamb. How are we to know this blood? By self-knowledge.

We were the earth where the standard of the cross was planted. We were the vessel that received the blood of the Lamb as it streamed from the cross. Why did we become that earth? Because the earth could not hold the cross upright, it refused to do so because it was so unjust; the nails could not have held the Lord fixed and nailed had not his ineffable love for our salvation held him there. It was love on fire with the glory of his Father and with desire for our salvation which fixed him to the cross. So we are the earth which held the cross upright and the vessel which received the blood.

We must live in simplicity, with neither pretensions nor mannerisms nor servile fear; we must walk in the light of a living faith that

shines in more than mere words; and always so, in adversity as well
as in prosperity, in times of persecution as well as in consolation.
Nothing will be able to change either the strength or the radiance of
our faith if the Truth has given us knowledge of truth nor just in
desire but in living experience.

—*St. Catherine*

MAY

MAY 1
St. Joseph the Worker

St. Joseph, by God's providence, was the one called upon to provide the ordinary necessities of life for God's Son and that Son's Mother by the labor of his hands.

Imagine who this Joseph must have been and what sort of man he must have been to have deserved to be honored by God—in keeping with the divine plan, of course—that he was called and believed to be the father of God himself. Imagine his worth from his very name which, as you probably know, means "increase." And remember, too, that great patriarch who was sold once into Egypt. Realize that the Joseph we are speaking of here not only shared that other great patriarch's name, but also imitated his chastity, closely resembling him in innocence and grace. The first Joseph, sold by jealous brothers and led off to Egypt, prefigured the selling of Christ. The second Joseph, fleeing jealous Herod, carried Christ away into Egypt. The first, keeping faith with the master, refused to couple with the mistress. The second, recognizing that his lady, the mother of the Lord, was a virgin, watched over her in faithful continence. The first had the gift of interpreting the hidden secrets of dreams; the second not only knew heavenly mysteries but even participated in them. The first Joseph stored up grain for himself and for all the people; the second was given charge of the bread that came down from heaven for his sake and for that of the whole world. There can be no doubt that this Joseph, to whom the mother of the Savior was engaged, was a good and faithful man. I tell you, he was the wise and faithful servant whom the Lord appointed to be the comfort of his mother and the bread-winner for his body. He was God's only and most faithful coadjutor in his great plan on earth.

—St. Bernard of Clairvaux

MAY 2
St. Athanasius

St. Athanasius (c. 297–373), archbishop of Alexandria, was forced into exile many times for his steadfast faith. He has left us many valuable theological treatises. Through the publication of his life of St. Anthony, he promoted the spread of monasticism in the West.

We do not worship a creature. Far be that from us! Such an error belongs to heathens and Arians. We worship the Lord of creation, Incarnate, the Word of God. For if the flesh also is in itself a part of the created world, yet it has become God's Body. And we neither divide the body from the Word and worship it by itself nor when we wish to worship the Word do we set him apart from the flesh, but knowing that "the Word was made flesh," we recognize him as God also after having come in the flesh.

—*St. Athanasius*

MAY 3
St. James

St. James (d. 62), son of Alphaeus, was an apostle of the Lord, to whom he was related by blood. He ruled over the Church in Jerusalem and wrote a canonical epistle before he died a martyr's death.

From James, the servant of God and of the Lord Jesus Christ. Greetings to the twelve tribes of the Dispersion.

My brothers and sisters, you will always have your trials but, when they come, try to treat them as happy privileges; you understand that your faith is only put to the test to make you patient, but patience too is to have its practical results so that you will become fully-developed, complete, with nothing missing.

If there is any one of you who needs wisdom, he must ask God, who gives to all freely and ungrudgingly; it will be given him. But he must ask with faith, and no trace of doubt, because a person who has doubts is like the waves thrown up in the sea when the wind drives. That sort of person, in two minds, wavering between different ways, must not expect that the Lord will give him anything.

—*St. James*

MAY 13
Blessed Julian of Norwich

Blessed Julian of Norwich (1342–1423) lived as an anchorite outside the church of St. Julian in Norwich, England, for over fifty years. She shared her experiences of God in her popular Revelations of Divine Love.

These Revelations were shewed to a simple creature that could no letter, in the year of our Lord 1373, the eighth day of May. . . . In this same time our Lord shewed me a ghostly sight of his homely loving. I saw that he is to us everything that is good and comfortable for us. He is our clothing that for love wrappeth us, claspeth us, and all becloseth us for tender love, that he may never leave us; being to us all that is good, as to mine understanding. . . . For as the body is clad in the cloth, and the flesh in the skin, and the bones in the flesh, and the heart in the whole, so are we, soul and flesh, clad in the Goodness of God, and enclosed. Yea, and more homely—for all these may waste and wear away, but the Goodness of God is ever whole—and more near to us, without any likeness; for truly our Lover desireth that our soul cleave to him with all its might, and that we be ever more cleaving to his Goodness. For of all things that heart may think, this pleaseth more God, and soonest speedeth the soul.

I say not this to them that be wise, for they know it well; but I say it to you that be simple, for ease and comfort; for we are all one in comfort. For soothly it was not shewed me that God loved me better than the least soul that is in grace; for I am sure that there be many that never had Shewing nor sight but of the common teaching of Holy Church that love God better than I. For if I look singularly to myself, I am right naught; but in general I am in hope, in oneness of charity with all mine even-Christians.

For in this oneness standeth the life of all mankind that shall be saved. For God is all that is good, as to my sight, and God hath made all that is made, and God loveth all that he hath made; and he that loveth generally all his even-Christians for God, he loveth all that is. For in mankind that shall be saved is comprehended all: that is to say, all that is made and the Maker of all. For in the human is God, and God is in all. And I hold by the grace of God he that beholdeth it thus shall be truly taught and mightily comforted, if he needeth comfort.

—Blessed Julian

MAY 14
St. Matthias

St. Matthias was chosen to replace Judas as one of the Twelve.

"In those days, Peter stood up in the midst of the disciples and said. . . ." As the fiery spirit to whom the flock was entrusted by Christ and as the leader in the band of apostles, Peter always took the initiative in speaking: "My brothers and sisters, we must choose from among our number." He left the decision to the whole body, at once augmenting the honor of those elected and avoiding suspicion of partiality.

Did not Peter then have the right to make the choice himself? Certainly he had the right, but he did not want to give the appearance of showing special favor to anyone. "And they nominated two," we read, "Joseph, who was called Barsabbas and surnamed Justus, and Matthias." He himself did not nominate them; all present did. But it was he who brought the issue forward, pointing out that it was not his own idea but had been suggested to him by a scriptural prophecy.

And they all prayed together, saying, "Lord, you know the human heart; make your choice known to us. You, not we." Appropriately they said that he knew the human heart, because the choice was to be made by him, not by others.

They spoke with such confidence, because someone had to be appointed. They did not say "choose" but "make known to us" the chosen one, "the one you choose," they said, fully aware that everything was being preordained by God.

—*St. John Chrysostom*

MAY 16
St. Simon Stock

St. Simon Stock (1165–1265) joined the Carmelites in Jerusalem and brought the order to England when the Moslems overran the Holy Land. From a vision of the Blessed Mother to him sprung the devotion and practice of the scapular.

O beautiful Flower of Carmel, most fruitful Vine, Splendor of Heaven, holy and singular, who brought forth the Son of God, still ever remaining a pure virgin, assist me in my necessities.

O Star of the Sea, help and protect me! Show me that you are my Mother.

—*St. Simon*

MAY 20
St. Bernardine

St. Bernardine (1380–1444), a humble Friar Minor but a powerful preacher, thrice refused the miter. He was known as a miracle worker.

When a fire is lit to clear a field, it burns off all the dry and useless weeds and thorns. When the sun rises and darkness is dispelled, robbers, night-prowlers and burglars hide away. So when Paul's voice was raised to preach the Gospel to the nations, like a great clap of thunder in the sky, his preaching was a blazing fire carrying all before it. It was the sun rising in full glory. Infidelity was consumed by it, false beliefs fled away, and the truth appeared like a great candle. By word of mouth, by letters, by miracles and by the example of his own life, Saint Paul bore the name of Jesus wherever he went. He praised the name of Jesus "at all times" but never more than when "bearing witness to his faith."

Moreover, the Apostle did indeed carry this name "before the Gentiles and kings and the sons of Israel" as a light to enlighten all nations. And this was his cry wherever he journeyed, "The night is passing away, the day is at hand. Let us cast off the works of darkness and put on the armor of light; let us conduct ourselves honorably as in the day." Paul himself showed forth the burning and shining light set upon a candle stick, everywhere proclaiming "Jesus and him crucified."

—St. Bernardine

MAY 24
St. Gregory VII

St. Gregory VII (1028–1085), the monk Hildebrand, was elected Pope in 1073 and inaugurated an extensive reform in the Church, renewing monastic life and bringing lay investiture to an end.

Now my dearest brethren, listen carefully to what I tell you. All those throughout the world who are numbered as Christians and who truly acknowledge the Christian faith know and believe that the blessed Peter, the prince of the Apostles, is the father of all Christians and, after Christ, the first shepherd, and that the holy Roman Church is the mother and teacher of all the churches. Therefore, if you believe this and hold to it without hesitation, I ask you by almighty God—I, your brother and unworthy teacher as I am—to support and assist your father and your mother if you wish to have, through them, the remission of all your sins, along with blessing and grace in this world and in the life to come.

—St. Gregory

MAY 25
St. Bede the Venerable

St. Bede the Venerable (672–735), who was brought to the monastery of Jarrow at the age of seven, spent his entire life in the study of Scripture, teaching and writing. He is considered the father of English historians as well as a Father of the Church and was declared a Doctor of the Church.

"You are a chosen race, a royal priesthood." This testimony of praise was given of old by Moses to God's ancient people. Now it is the nations to whom Peter the Apostle gives this title, because they have believed in Christ who, like a cornerstone, gathers the nations into the salvation which was formerly meant for Israel. He calls those nations "a chosen race" on account of their faith, to distinguish them from those who on rejecting the cornerstone were themselves rejected. He calls them "a royal priesthood" because they are joined to the body of him who is the sovereign king and true priest. As king he confers his kingdom on them and as priest he purges away their sins by the sacrifice of his blood. They are called "a royal priesthood," because, recollecting the hope of the eternal kingdom, they ceaselessly offer to God the sacrifice of a blameless life.

They are called "a holy nation, God's own people" in accordance with Paul's words concerning the oracle of prophecy: "My righteous one shall live by faith, and if he shrinks back, my will has no pleasure in him. But we are not of those who shrink back and are destroyed, but of those who have faith and keep their souls."

Peter recalls the mystery of the old story and he shows that it has found its fulfillment in the new people of God: "That you may declare the wonderful deeds of him who called you out of darkness into his marvelous light." For just as those who were freed by Moses from

Egyptian slavery singing a joyful song of triumph after the crossing of the Red Sea and the submerging of Pharaoh's Egyptians—who afflicted God's people and whose name means darkness and misfortune—are a true figure of us whose sins pursue us but are washed away in baptism, the deliverance of the children of Israel and their journey to the land promised to them of old corresponds to the mystery of our redemption. We are making our way towards the light of our celestial home, illumined and guided by Christ's grace. This light of grace was prefigured by the pillar of cloud and fire which protected the children of Israel from the darkness of night throughout their journey, and brought them by wonderful ways to the promised destination, the inhabiting of their own land.

—St. Bede the Venerable

MAY 26
St. Augustine
of Canterbury

St. Augustine of Canterbury (d. 605), a monk from the same monastery as Pope St. Gregory the Great, was sent by him to evangelize Britain. He was very successful and established a monastery at Canterbury and several Episcopal sees.

Who, my dear Brother, is capable of describing the great joy of believers when they have learned what the grace of Almighty God and your own cooperation achieved among the Angles? They abandoned the errors of darkness and were bathed with the light of holy faith. With full awareness, they trampled on the idols which they had previously adored with savage fear. They are now committed to Almighty God. They bow down to the ground in prayer lest their minds cling too closely to earthly things. Whose achievement is this? It is the achievement of him who said, "My Father is at work until now and I am at work as well."

—*St. Gregory the Great*

MAY 30
Feast of the
Immaculate Heart of Mary

This feast seeks to honor the immense purity and love that God created in the heart of his Mother, the Blessed Virgin Mary.

There is no doubt that whatever we say in praise of the mother touches the Son and when we honor her Son we detract nothing from the mother's glory. For if, as Solomon says, "A wise son is the glory of his father," how much more glorious is it to become the mother of Wisdom himself? But how can I attempt to praise her whom the prophets have proclaimed, the angel has acknowledged and the evangelist has described as praiseworthy?

—*St. Bernard of Clairvaux*

MAY 31

Feast of the Visitation
of the Blessed Virgin Mary

*When Gabriel told Mary of her cousin's pregnancy, Mary went in
haste to help her.*

"My soul proclaims the greatness of the Lord, and my spirit rejoices
in God my savior." With these words Mary first acknowledges the
special gifts she has been given.

Above all the saints, she alone could truly rejoice in Jesus, her
savior, for she knew that he who was the source of eternal salvation
would be born in time in her body, in one person both her own Son
and the Lord.

"For the Almighty has done great things for me, and holy is his
name." Mary attributes nothing to her own merits. She refers all her
greatness to the gift of one whose essence is power and whose nature
is greatness, for he fills with greatness and strength the small and the
weak who believe in him.

She did well to add "and holy is his name," to warn those who
heard, and indeed all who would receive his words, that they must
believe and call upon his name. For they too could share in everlasting holiness and true salvation according to the words of the
prophet, "And it will come to pass, that everyone who calls on the
name of the lord will be saved." This is the name she spoke of earlier
when she said "and my spirit rejoices in God my savior."

—St. Bede the Venerable

JUNE

JUNE 1
St. Justin Martyr

St. Justin Martyr (c. 100–c. 165), a pagan philosopher converted to Christ, courageously and effectively wrote and debated in defense of the faith, winning himself a martyr's crown.

The food that is called among us "Eucharist" no one is allowed to partake of except the one who believes that the things which we teach are true, and who has been washed with the washing that is for the remission of sins, and for regeneration and who is living in the way that Christ enjoined. For we do not receive these as common bread and common drink, but as we have been taught: that Jesus Christ our Savior, having been made flesh by the Word of God had both flesh and blood for our salvation; and that the food which is blessed by the prayer of his word, and from which our flesh and blood by transmutation are nourished, is the flesh and blood of Jesus who was made flesh. For the apostles, in the memoirs which are composed by them and are called Gospels, have thus delivered to us what was enjoined upon them: that Jesus took bread, and when he had given thanks he said, "This do in remembrance of me, this is my body" and that after the same manner, having taken the cup and given thanks, he said, "This is my blood" and gave it to them alone.

We continually remind each other of these things. And the wealthy among us help the needy and we always keep together and for all things wherewith we are supplied, we bless the Maker of all through his Son Jesus Christ, and through the Holy Spirit. And on the day called Sunday, all who live in cities or in the country gather together in one place, and the memoirs of the apostles or the writings of the prophets are read, as long as the time permits; then, when the reader has ceased, the president verbally instructs and exhorts to the imitation of these good things. Then we all rise together and pray and as we said before, when our prayer is ended, bread and wine and water are brought, and the president in like manner offers prayers and thanksgivings, according to his ability, and the people assent, saying, "Amen." There is a distribution to each and a participation of that over which thanks have been given, and to those who are absent a portion is sent by the deacons. And they who are well to do and willing, give what each thinks fit. And what is collected is deposited with the president, who succors the orphans and widows, and those who through sickness or any other cause are in want and those who are in bonds and the strangers sojourning among us and in a word takes care of all who are in need.

Sunday is the day on which we all hold our common assembly, because it is the first day on which God, having wrought a change in the darkness and matter, made the world and Jesus Christ our Savior on the same day rose from the dead.

—*St. Justin*

JUNE 5
St. Boniface

St. Boniface (673–754), an English monk, established monastic life in Germany as the center of a powerful missionary outreach. Boniface, who had been ordained bishop by Pope Gregory II, crowned his life with a martyr's death.

Let us stand fast in what is right and prepare our souls for trial. Let us wait upon God's strengthening aid and say to him, "O Lord, you have been our refuge in all generations."

Let us trust in him who has placed this burden upon us. What we ourselves cannot bear let us bear with the help of Christ. For he is all-powerful and he tells us, "My yoke is easy and my burden is light."

Let us continue to fight on the day of the Lord. The days of anguish and of tribulation have overtaken us. If God so wills, let us die for the holy laws of our fathers, so that we may deserve to obtain an eternal inheritance with them.

—*St. Boniface*

JUNE 9
St. Ephrem

St. Ephrem (c. 306–c. 393), a deacon, wrote voluminously in Syriac on exegetical, dogmatic, and ascetical themes, drawing heavily on scriptural sources. He became a Doctor of the Church, and his hymns won for him the name "Harp of the Holy Spirit."

In your sacrament we daily embrace you and receive you into our bodies. Make us worthy to experience the resurrection for which we hope. We have had your treasure hidden within us ever since we received baptismal grace. It grows ever richer at your sacramental table.

Teach us to find our joy in your favor, Lord. We have within us your memorial, received at your spiritual table. Let us possess it in its full reality when all things shall be made new.

—*St. Ephrem*

JUNE 13
St. Anthony of Padua

St. Anthony of Padua (1195–1231), "Wonder Worker," "Hammer of Heretics," "Patron of the Poor," was the greatest preacher of his times.

One who is filled with the Holy Spirit speaks in different languages. These different languages are different ways of witnessing to Christ, such as humility, poverty, patience, and obedience. We speak in these languages when we reveal in ourselves these virtues to others. Actions speak louder than words; let your words teach and your actions speak.

—*St. Anthony*

JUNE 14
Blessed Gerard of Clairvaux

Blessed Gerard of Clairvaux (1089–1138), St. Bernard's older brother, followed him to Citeaux and then to Clairvaux, where he was a constant support and intimate advisor.

You are aware, my dear Brothers, that a loyal companion has left me alone on the pathway of life; he who was so alert to my needs, so enterprising at work, so agreeable in his ways. Who was ever so necessary to me? Who ever loved me as he? My brother by blood, but bound to me more intimately by religious profession. Share my mourning with me, you who know these things. I was frail in body, and he sustained me, faint in heart and he gave me courage, slothful and negligent and he spurred me on, forgetful and improvident and he gave me timely warning. Why was he torn from me? Why snatched from my embraces, a man of one mind with me, a man according to my heart? We loved each other in life. . . .

—St. Bernard of Clairvaux

JUNE 19
St. Romuald

St. Romuald (c. 950–1027) entered a monastery at twenty but left three years later to embrace an eremitical life. Through the years others joined him and he founded other hermitages. The five he established at Camaldoli united to form an order, living under the modification of the Benedictine rule which he had formulated.

Romuald lived in the vicinity of the city of Parenzo for three years. In the first year he built a monastery and appointed an abbot with monks. For the next two years he remained there in seclusion.

Where the holy man might arrange to live, he would follow the same pattern. First he would build an oratory with an altar in a cell; then he would shut himself in and forbid access.

Finally, after he had lived in many places, perceiving that his end was near, he returned to the monastery he had built in the valley of Castor. While he awaited with certainty his approaching death, he ordered a cell to be constructed there with an oratory in which he might isolate himself and preserve silence until death.

Accordingly the hermitage was built, since he had made up his mind that he would die there. His body began to grow more and more oppressed by affliction and was already failing. One day he began to feel the loss of his physical strength under all the harassment of increasingly violent affliction. As the sun was beginning to set, he instructed two monks who were standing by to go out and close the door of the cell behind them. They were to come back to him at daybreak to celebrate matins. They were so concerned about his end that they went out reluctantly and did not rest immediately. On the contrary, since they were worried that their master might die, they lay hidden near the cell and watched this precious treasure. For some time they continued to listen attentively until they heard neither movement nor sound. Rightly guessing what had happened, they pushed open the door, rushed in quickly, lit a candle, and found the holy man lying on his back, his blessed soul snatched up into heaven.

—St. Peter Damian

JUNE 21
St. Aloysius Gonzaga

St. Aloysius Gonzaga (1568–1591), born of a noble family, entered the Jesuits at seventeen. He died six years later while ministering to the victims of the plague.

May the comfort and grace of the Holy Spirit be yours forever, most honored lady. Your letter found me lingering still in this region of the dead, but now I must rouse myself to make my way to heaven at last and to praise God forever in the land of the living. Indeed, I had hoped that before this time my journey there would have been over. If charity, as Saint Paul said, means "to weep with those who weep and rejoice with those who are glad," then, dearest mother, you shall rejoice exceedingly that God in his grace and his love for you is showing me the path to true happiness and assuring me that I shall ever love him.

Take care above all things, most honored lady, not to insult God's boundless loving kindness. You would certainly do this if you mourned as dead one living face to face with God, one whose prayers can bring you in your troubles more powerful aid that they ever could on earth. And our parting will not be for long; we shall see each other again in heaven; we shall be united with our Savior. There

we shall praise him with heart and soul, sing his mercies forever and
enjoy eternal happiness.

—*St. Aloysius*

JUNE 22
St. Thomas More

*St. Thomas More (1478–1535), a brilliant Christian humanist, gave
up his post as Lord Chancellor of England and suffered imprisonment and death rather than betray his loyalty to the Pope: "the
King's good servant but God's first."*

Your daughterly, loving letter, my dearly beloved child, was and is, I
faithfully assure you, of much greater inward comfort to me than my
pen can adequately express, because of the many things that I noted
in it, but of all things, most especially, that God of his great goodness
gives you the grace to consider the incomparable difference between
the wretched estate of this present life and the splendid estate of the
life to come, for those who die in God and to pray God in such good
Christian fashion that it may please him. It does me good to repeat
your own words: "Of his tender pity so firmly to rest our love in him,
with little regard for this world, and so to flee from sin and embrace
virtue, that we may say with Saint Paul, 'To me to live is Christ and
to die is gain.' And likewise, 'My desire is to depart and be with
Christ.' "

I beseech our Lord, my dearly beloved daughter, that it may
please him to give to your father the grace daily to remember and to
pray the wholesome prayer that he has put into your mind, and to
you yourself who have written it, likewise devoutly to kneel and to
pray it daily. For surely if God gives us that, he gives us and will give
us, with it, all that we can duly wish.

That you fear your own frailty, Margaret, in no way displeases me.

God gave to both of us the grace to despair of our own self and wholly to depend and hang upon the hope and strength of God. The blessed apostle Saint Paul found such a lack of strength in himself that in his own temptation he had three times to call upon and cry out before God, to take that temptation from him and yet he did not succeed in his prayer in the manner that he wanted. God answered him: "My grace is sufficient for you," giving him the certainty that, however feeble and faint he himself might be, and however likely to fall, yet the grace of God was sufficient to keep him upright and to enable him to stand. And our Lord said further: "My power is made perfect in weakness." The meeker a person is, the more is the strength of God declared in safeguarding him. And so, Saint Paul says: "I can do all things in him who strengthens me."

And verily, my dear daughter, in this is my great comfort, that although by nature I so shrink from pain that I am almost afraid I have gone through [the pain]—and before coming here (as I have already revealed to you) I suffered some that were neither small nor few in number—with a heavy and a fearful heart, anticipating all such perils and painful deaths as might befall me, and lying restless and awake for long hours while my wife thought I slept, yet in such fears and apprehensions (I thank the mighty mercy of God) I never in my mind, in order to endure the uttermost, had any intention to consent, to do anything that in my conscience—with other men's it is not for me to meddle—I would think to be such as to cast me, to my damnation, into the displeasure of God.

And this is the last point to which any concerned with salvation may come, as far as I can see, each being required if he discerns some peril, to examine his conscience surely by learning and by good counsel, and to be sure that his conscience be such as to conform with his salvation or else to reform it. And if the matter be such that both sides of the question conform to salvation, then on which ever side his conscience falls he is safe enough before God. Therefore I firmly thank our Lord that my own conscience conforms with my own salvation. I beseech our Lord to bring all to his bliss.

—St. Thomas

JUNE 23
St. Paulinus of Nola

> *St. Paulinus of Nola (355–431) was a happily married man, a
> wealthy governor, and a talented poet and writer. In 389 he and his
> wife, Therasia, were baptized, gave their wealth to the poor, and
> embraced a monastic style of life, offering generous hospitality to all
> who came.*

I give thanks and boast in the Lord, who, one and the same throughout the world, produces his love in his people through the Holy
Spirit whom he pours out upon all flesh.

But you should know everything about me and you should be
aware that I am a sinner of long standing. It is not so long ago that
"I was led out of darkness and the shadow of death." Only recently
have I begun to breathe the air of life; only recently have I put my
hand to the plough and taken up the cross of Christ.

—*St. Paulinus*

JUNE 24
Birth of
St. John the Baptist

St. John, cousin of the Lord, was the fruit of a miraculous concep-
tion in his parents' old age and was sanctified in the womb.

The Church observes the birth of John as a hallowed event. We have
no such commemoration for any other of the fathers. But it is significant that we celebrate the birthdays of John and of Jesus. This day
cannot be passed by. And even if my explanation does not match the
dignity of the feast, you may still meditate on it with great depth and
profit.

John appears as the boundary between the two testaments, the
new and the old. That he is a sort of boundary the Lord himself
bears witness, when he speaks of "the Law and the prophets up until
John the Baptist." Thus he represents times past and is the herald of
the new era to come. As a representative of the past he is born of
aged parents; as a herald of the new era, he is declared to be a
prophet while still in his mother's womb. For when yet unborn he
leapt in his mother's womb at the arrival of blessed Mary. In that
womb he had already been designated a prophet, even before he was
born; it was revealed that he was to be Christ's precursor, before they
ever saw one another. These are divine happenings, going beyond the
limits of your human frailty.

When John was preaching the Lord's coming he was asked "Who
are you?" And he replied, "I am the voice of one crying in the
wilderness." The voice is John, but the Lord "in the beginning was

the Word." John was a voice that lasted only for a time; Christ, the
Word from the beginning, is eternal.

—*St. Augustine*

JUNE 25
St. Prosper of Aquitane

*St. Prosper of Aquitane (c. 390–c. 465), a married layman, was a
friend of St. Hilary and served as secretary to Pope St. Leo. He left
us his own heritage of deeply spiritual writings.*

The evidence from Scripture demonstrates abundantly, I think, that
the faith which justifies a sinner cannot be had except for God's gift,
and that it is not a reward for previous merits. Rather, it is given that
it may be a source of merit and while it is itself given unprayed for,
the prayers it inspires obtain all other favors.

—*St. Prosper*

JUNE 27
St. Cyril of Alexandria

St. Cyril of Alexandria (370–444), a native of Alexandria, succeeded his uncle as archbishop of that city. He is best known for his role at the Council of Ephesus, where the Blessed Virgin's divine maternity was solemnly proclaimed.

That anyone could doubt the right of the holy Virgin to be called the Mother of God fills me with astonishment. Surely she must be the Mother of God if our Lord Jesus Christ is God and she gave birth to him! Our Lord's disciples may not have used those exact words, but they delivered to us the belief those words enshrine and this has also been taught us by the holy fathers.

The divinely inspired Scriptures affirm that the Word of God was made flesh, that is to say, he was united to a human body endowed with a rational soul. He undertook to help the descendants of Abraham, fashioning a body for himself from a woman and sharing our flesh and blood, to enable us to see in him not only God, but also, by reason of this union, a man like ourselves.

It is held, therefore, that there is in Emmanuel two entities, divinity and humanity. Yet our Lord Jesus Christ is nonetheless one, the one true Son, both God and man; not a deified man on the same footing as those who share the divine nature by grace, but true God who for our sake appeared in human form. We are assured of this by Saint Paul's declaration, "When the fullness of time came, God sent his Son, born of a woman, born under the law, to redeem those who were under the law and to enable us to be adopted as sons."

—St. Cyril

JUNE 28
St. Irenaeus

St. Irenaeus (c. 125–c. 203), bishop of Lyons, was a disciple of a disciple of St. John the Evangelist. He wrote several powerful apologetic works.

Those who see God will partake of life, for the splendor of God is life-giving. Such is the motive with which he who is indiscernible, incomprehensible and invisible offers himself to be seen, comprehended and discerned by us: in order that he may give life to those who discern him and see him. For, if his greatness is inscrutable, his kindness also is inexpressible and it is out of his kindness that he reveals himself and gives life to those who see him. It is impossible to live without life, and there is no life except by taking part in God, a partaking which consists in seeing God and enjoying his kindness.

We will see God in order to live, becoming immortal through what we have seen, attaining to God. This is what the Prophet proclaimed in figurative speech, that God would be seen by those who carry his Spirit within them and wait unceasingly for him to come, as Moses said in Deuteronomy: "We have this day seen God speak with us and we still live."

God, who brings about all things, is invisible and inexpressible, both as to his power and as to his greatness, for all those whom he had made. None the less, he is not entirely unknown to them, for all come to know, through his Word, that there is only God, the Father, who controls all things and gives existence to all this, as the Lord said: "No one has ever seen God; the only Son, who is in the bosom of the Father, he has made it known."

Thus from the beginning the Son is the Revealer of the Father.

—St. Irenaeus

JUNE 29
St. Peter and St. Paul

St. Peter and St. Paul, apostles who suffered for Christ at Rome: Peter chosen by Christ to lead the apostolic band; Paul, to be added to it to lead the outreach to the Gentiles.

From Simon Peter, servant and apostle of Jesus Christ, to all who treasure the same faith as ourselves, given through the righteousness of our God and Savior Jesus Christ. May you have more and more grace and peace as you come to know our Lord more and more.

By his divine power, he has given us all the things that we need for life and for true devotion, bringing us to know God himself, who has called us by his own glory and goodness. In making these gifts, he has given us the guarantee of something very great and wonderful to come: through them you will be able to share the divine nature. . . .

But to attain this, you will have to do your utmost yourselves, adding goodness to the faith you have, understanding to your goodness, self-control to your understanding, patience to your self-control, true devotion to your patience, kindness toward your fellow men to your devotion and, to this kindness, love. If you have a generous supply of these, they will not leave you ineffectual or unproductive—they will bring you to a real knowledge of our Lord Jesus Christ.

—St. Peter

JULY

JULY 3
St. Thomas

St. Thomas (first century) apostle of the Lord, is believed to have brought the Good News to southern India, where he suffered martyrdom.

Touching Christ, Thomas cried out: "My Lord and my God." Jesus said to him: "Because you have seen me, Thomas, you have believed." Paul said: "Faith is the guarantee of things hoped for, the evidence of things unseen." It is clear, then, that faith is the proof of what cannot be seen. What is seen gives knowledge, not faith. When Thomas saw and touched, why was he told: "You have believed because you have seen me"? Because what he saw and what he believed were different things. God cannot be seen by mortal man. Thomas saw a human being, whom he acknowledged to be God, and said: "My Lord and my God." Seeing, he believed; looking at one who was true man, he cried out that this was God, the God he could not see.

—St. Gregory the Great

JULY 4
St. Odo of Canterbury

*St. Odo of Canterbury (d. 959), though born in East Anglia, entered
the French monastery of Fleury-sur-Loire. He was later named
bishop of Ramsberry and then archbishop of Canterbury (942).*

In the Gospel, Jesus is described as having been received by two
sisters, one of whom served him while the other one devoted herself
to listening to his words. It is customary to see in these two women
mentioned in Scripture two ways of the Church: Martha represented
the active life, and Mary the contemplative life. Martha was toiling
over works of mercy; Mary was still and watchful. The active is
given over to love of neighbor, the contemplative to love of God.
Now Christ is God and man. And he was enfolded in the unique love
of the Blessed Virgin Mary, whether she served his humanity or
whether she was absorbed in contemplation of his divinity. A wise
man called Mary "the philosopher of the Christians" and this word,
philosopher, means "love of wisdom." In fact, on the one hand
Christians should delight in finding true wisdom in Mary; on the
other hand Mary found delight in Christ who is the true Wisdom of
Christians. She delighted at all times and more than anyone else both
in serving his humanity and in contemplating his divinity.

Others serve Christ's members; Mary served Christ in person—
Christ himself, the Son of God and her son—and not only, as did
Martha, through outward works but with her own substance. She
offered to him the hospitality of her own womb. In his tender infancy
she helped the weakness of his humanity, caressing him, bathing
him, caring for him. She carried him to Egypt, fleeing from Herod's
persecution and brought him back again. Finally, after the manifold
services of a Martha, she stood close to him when he died on the

cross; she assisted at his burial and she suffered so greatly then that, in accordance with Simeon's prophecy, her soul was pierced by the sharp sword of sorrow. Thus she was Martha and who could equal her in service?

In contemplation too, in Mary's role, she excels everyone. In truth, how could she not have been contemplative, she who bore within her the very Divinity, one with her flesh in the Person of the Son of God. This Word who was with God in the beginning, and who was God, it was he whom she bore. Then she listened to him, spoke with him, played with him, contemplated him. "Christ the power of God and the wisdom of God" was in Mary. From henceforth were found in her all the power and wisdom of God. "In Christ are hid all the treasures of wisdom and knowledge." All the fullness of the Divinity was found corporally in Christ. He was in Mary, that is why all the fullness of the Divinity was in Mary. Then the Father is in Mary, the Son is in Mary, and the Holy Spirit is in Mary. Such was Mary the contemplative, she who, in the only Son of God whom she bore in her flesh, contemplated the glory of the whole Trinity.

—*St. Odo*

JULY 5
St. Anthony Zaccaria

St. Anthony Zaccaria (1502–1539), in the course of a very short and fruitful ministry, founded the Barnabites or Clerics of Saint Paul.

"We are fools for Christ's sake"—our holy guide and most revered patron, Paul, was speaking about himself and the rest of the apostles and about the other people who profess the Christian and apostolic way of life. We should love and feel compassion for those who opposed us, rather than abhor and despise them, since they are themselves and do us good and adorn us with crowns of everlasting glory while they incite God's anger against themselves. And even more than this, we should pray for them and not be overcome by evil, but overcome evil by goodness. We should heap good works "like hot coals" of burning love "upon their heads," as our Apostle urges us to do, so that when they become aware of our tolerance and gentleness, they may undergo a change of heart and be prompted to turn in love to God.

In his mercy God has chosen us, unworthy as we are, out of this world to serve him and thus to advance in goodness and to bear the greatest possible purity of love in patience.

—*St. Anthony*

JULY 15
St. Bonaventure

St. Bonaventure (1218–1274), the Seraphic Doctor, was an outstand-ing teacher of Scripture and theology at Paris until his election as minister general of the Franciscan order in 1257.

Prayer consists in turning the mind to God. Do you wish to know how to turn your mind toward God? Follow my words. When you pray gather up your whole self, enter with your Beloved into the chamber of your heart, and there remain alone with him, forgetting all exterior concerns. And so rise aloft with all your love and all your mind, your affections, your desires, and devotion. And let not your mind wander away from your prayer, but rise again and again in the fervor of your piety until you enter into the place of the wonderful tabernacle, even the house of God. There your heart will be delighted at the sight of your Beloved and you will taste and see how good the Lord is and how great is his goodness.

—St. Bonaventure

JULY 16
Our Lady of Mount Carmel

According to tradition, Mary, the Mother of Jesus, under the title of Our Lady of Mount Carmel, appeared to a superior of the Carmelite Order in 1272 and gave him a scapular with assurances of special care for those who would wear it as a sign of placing themselves under her protection.

Take this scapular. Whosoever dies wearing it shall not suffer eternal fire. It shall be a sign of salvation, a protection in danger, and a pledge of peace.

—Our Lady of Mount Carmel

JULY 21
St. Lawrence of Brindisi

St. Lawrence of Brindisi (1559–1619) was a Capuchin noted for his preaching.

There is a spiritual life that we share with the angels in heaven and with the divine spirits, for like them we have been formed in the image and likeness of God. The bread that is necessary for living this life is the grace of the Holy Spirit and the love of God. But grace and love are nothing without faith, since without faith it is impossible to please God. "Faith comes through hearing." And what is heard is the Word of Christ. The preaching of the Word of God, then, is necessary for the spiritual life, just as the planting of seed is necessary for bodily life.

The Word of God is light to the mind and fire to the will. It enables us to know God and to love him. Against the hardness of a heart that persists in wrongdoing, it acts as a hammer. Against the world, the flesh and the devil it serves as a sword that destroys all sin.

—*St. Lawrence*

JULY 22
St. Mary Magdalene

Honored by the Eastern Church as "Equal to the Apostles," St. Mary Magdalene was freed from diabolical domination by the Lord and became the first herald of the resurrection.

When Mary Magdalene came to the tomb and did not find the Lord's body, she thought it had been taken away and so informed the disciples. After they came and saw the tomb, they too believed what Mary had told them. The text then says: "The disciples went back home," and it adds: "but Mary wept and remained standing outside the tomb."

We should reflect on Mary's attitude and the great love she felt for Christ; for though the disciples had left the tomb, she remained. She was still seeking the one she had not found, and while she sought she wept; burning with the fire of love, she longed for him whom she thought had been taken away. And so it happened that the woman who stayed behind to seek Christ was the only one to see him. For perseverance is essential to any good deed, as the voice of truth tells us: "Whoever perseveres to the end will be saved."

—*St. Gregory the Great*

JULY 23
St. Bridget

St. Bridget (1303–1373), mother of eight, went from the court to found the austere religious Order of the Most Holy Trinity (Bridgettines). She wrote extensively of her mystical experiences.

Eternal praise to you, my Lord Jesus Christ, for the time you endured on the cross the greatest torments and sufferings for us sinners. The sharp pain of your wounds fiercely penetrated even to your blessed soul and cruelly pierced your most sacred heart till finally you sent forth your spirit in peace, bowed your head and humbly commended yourself into the hands of God your Father, and your whole body remained cold in death.

Blessed may you be, my Lord Jesus Christ. For our salvation you allowed your side and heart to be pierced with a lance and from that side water and your precious blood flowed out abundantly for our redemption.

Unending honor be to you, my Lord Jesus Christ. On the third day you rose from the dead and appeared to those you have chosen. And after forty days you ascended into heaven before the eyes of many witnesses and then in heaven you gathered together in glory those you love, whom you had freed from hell.

Rejoicing and eternal praise be to you, my Lord Jesus Christ, who sent the Holy Spirit into the hearts of your disciples and increased the boundless love of God in their spirits. Blessed are you and praiseworthy and glorious forever, my Lord Jesus.

—St. Bridget

JULY 25
St. James

St. James (d. c. 42), the son of Zebedee and brother of St. John, was put to death as a disciple of Christ by King Herod.

The sons of Zebedee press Christ: "Promise that one may sit at your right side and the other at your left." What does he do? He wants to show them that it is not a spiritual gift for which they are asking, and that if they knew what their request involved, they would never dare make it. So he says: "You do not know what you are asking," that is, what a great and splendid thing it is and how much beyond the reach even of the heavenly powers. Then he continues: "Can you drink the cup which I must drink and be baptized with the baptism which I must undergo?" He is saying, "You talk of sharing honors and rewards with me, but I must talk of struggle and toil. Now is not the time for rewards or the time for my glory to be revealed. Earthly life is the time for bloodshed, war and danger."

The disciples do not know what they are saying. How does Christ reply: "You will indeed drink my cup and be baptized with my baptism." Thus, after lifting their minds to higher goals and preparing them to meet and overcome all that will make them desolate, he sets them straight on their request.

—St. John Chrysostom

JULY 26
St. Anne and St. Joachim

Tradition gives these names to the parents of the Blessed Virgin Mary. God in his providence must have prepared this couple with special grace for their parenting. The immaculate conception took place in St. Anne; St. Joachim's love cooperated with God in bringing Mary into existence.

Today we give thanks for the parents of the Mother of God. They are at the very beginning of the salvation of us all, and their festival is therefore also the festival of their daughter. It is the moment at which to exclaim: The Lord has blessed the house of King David because of his distant descendant, Mary, Mother of Life. He has blessed the house of the righteous Joachim and Anne because of their holy daughter, Mary, Mother of Christ and Mother of God.

Thrice happy are the parents of the Mother of God! The whole world is in their debt: the prophets because thanks to them, the prophecies which they uttered concerning the incarnation of Christ have been fulfilled; the apostles because thanks to their daughter, they have become sons of light; the holy martyrs because to them they owe their crown; the holy and the righteous because they will be able to inherit good things that are to come; sinners because the prayers of the Mother will obtain mercy for them. Let us, too, loudly and gratefully say to them:

Rejoice, Joachim, most venerable father of her who after God is our hope. Rejoice, Anne, most honorable mother of the Mother of our Life.

Rejoice, Father! You are the good sower, the cultivator of a fertile field. Rejoice, most fruitful Mother! You are the root of our salvation.

Rejoice, Father! You are the grower of the vine which gave the good grape. Rejoice, Mother! You are the favored field of the good earth.

Rejoice Father! You planted the spiritual paradise. Rejoice, Mother! You are the tree which bears a faultless branch.

Rejoice, Father! You are the case which encloses the flawless pearl. Rejoice, Mother! You are the rock which contains the most pure emerald.

Rejoice, Father! You are the stream from which the well-spring of life gushed forth. Rejoice, Mother! You are the pitcher from which all thirst for offspring is quenched.

Our mouth is filled with praises for your wonderful holiness. But we are incapable of celebrating as we should your conjugal union in which God has united you; we could do so only by borrowing the voice of Christ, your grandson, according to the flesh, to bless you both in saying to you, "Rejoice and be glad, for your reward, which is the fruit of your flesh, is great in heaven."

—Blessed Cosmas

JULY 29
Mary, Martha, and Lazarus

The Gospels tell us of this family whose home was a special place of hospitality for our Blessed Lord.

Let us consider how rightly ordered charity has distributed these three spiritual employments in this house of ours, allotting to Martha the external administration, to Mary interior contemplation, and the practice of penance to Lazarus. It is true, all three occupations are found united in every perfect soul; nevertheless, different souls seem to be intended more particularly for different functions, some being called to the repose of prayer, others to the exercise of charity towards their brothers and sisters, others again to the practice of penance, recounting all their years in the bitterness of their souls, like the slain sleeping in the sepulchres. Such a division appears to be plainly necessary, so that Mary's mind may be occupied with loving and lofty sentiments of her God, Martha's with the kind and compassionate thoughts of her neighbor, and that the mind of Lazarus may think of nothing but his own misery and abjection. Let each one consider to which of these grades he belongs.

—St. Bernard of Clairvaux

JULY 30
St. Peter Chrysologus

St. Peter Chrysologus (406–c.450), the "Golden Mouthed," was bishop of Revenna. His extant homilies won for him the title of Doctor of the Church.

When God saw the world overturned by fear, he sent forth his love to recall the world to himself, his grace, to invite the world to come to him; his affection, to embrace it. At the Flood his vengeance purified the world from an inveterate ill. He called Noah to engender a new world, encouraged him with gentle words, gave him his intimate trust, instructed him with kindness concerning the future. Rather than giving him orders, he took part in Noah's labor and enclosed in the ark the seed of the whole world, so that the love contained in his covenant might banish fear of slavery and so that a communion of love might preserve what labor in common had saved.

God called Abraham from the midst of the nations, he magnified his name and made him the father of believers. He went with him on his way, protected him from the foreigner, piled riches on him, honored him with victories, assured him of this promise, snatched him from injustices, consoled him in his hospitality, and amazed him with an unhoped-for birth, so that, overwhelmed with all his wealth, drawn by the great sweetness of divine love, he learned to love God and no longer to fear him, to adore him in loving him and no longer in trembling.

Later, when Jacob was in flight, God consoled him with dreams. On his return God challenged him to combat and in the battle he clasped Jacob in his arms so that he loved the Father of battles and no longer feared him. Then God called Moses and spoke to him with a father's love, calling him to deliver his people.

In all these events the flame of divine love enkindled the human heart, the rapture of the love of God was infused into the tenderest felling of human hearts; and they, wounded in soul, began to long to see God with the eyes of flesh. If the world cannot contain God, how could the limited gaze of a human person contain him? But love is not ruled by what must be, nor by what is possible. Love knows nothing of this law; it has no rule, it knows no bounds.

He took flesh that we might see him.

—*St. Peter*

JULY 31
St. Ignatius of Loyola

St. Ignatius of Loyola (1491–1556), the thirteenth child of a noble Spanish couple, was a soldier of fortune before the blessing of a severe wound gave him time to examine his life and turn to Christ, for whom he founded a powerful army, the Society of Jesus.

Lord, I freely yield all my freedom to you. Take my memory, my intellect, and my entire will. You have given me anything I am or have; I give it all back to you to stand under your will alone. Your love and your grace are enough for me; I shall ask for nothing more.

—*St. Ignatius*

AUGUST

AUGUST 1
St. Alphonsus Liguori

St. Alphonsus Liguori (1696–1787), a lawyer, became a priest and then founded the Congregation of the Most Holy Redeemer. He served briefly as a bishop but was more interested in writing and preaching.

All holiness and perfection of life lies in our love for Jesus Christ our God, who is our redeemer and our supreme good.

Has not God in fact won for himself a claim on all our love? From all eternity he has loved us. And it is in this vein that he speaks to us: "O friend, consider carefully that I first loved you. You had not yet appeared in the light of day, nor did the world yet exist, but already I loved you. From all eternity I have loved you."

Since God knew that we are enticed by favors, he wished to bind us to his love by means of his gifts: I want to catch you with snares, those chains of love in which you allow yourselves to be entrapped, so that you will love me. All the gifts which he bestowed on us were given to this end. He gave us a soul, made in his likeness. He endowed us with memory, intellect and will; he gave us a body equipped with the senses. It was for us that he created heaven and earth and such an abundance of things. He made all these things out of love for us, so that all creation might serve us and we in turn might love God out of gratitude for so many gifts.

But he did not wish to give us only beautiful creatures, the truth is that to win for himself our love, he went so far as to bestow upon us the fullness of himself. The eternal Father went so far as to give us his only Son. When he saw that we were all dead through sin and deprived of his grace, what did he do? He sent his beloved Son to make reparation for us and to call us back to a sinless life.

—*St. Alphonsus*

AUGUST 2
St. Eusebius of Vercelli

St. Eusebius of Vercelli (c. 283–371), a native of Sardinia, was the first Western bishop to unite monastic and clerical life. He suffered exile in defense of the Faith.

Dearly Beloved,

I rejoice in your faith, in the salvation that comes from faith, in your good works, which are not confined to your own surroundings but spread far and wide. Like a farmer tending a sound tree, untouched by ax or fire because of its fruit, I want not only to serve you in the body, good people that you are, but also to give my life for your well-being.

So I beg you to keep the faith with all vigilance, to preserve harmony, to be earnest in prayer, to remember me always, so that the Lord may grant freedom to his Church which is suffering throughout the world and that I may be set free from the sufferings that weigh upon me, and so be able to rejoice with you.

—St. Eusebius

AUGUST 3
St. Hippolytus

St. Hippolytus (d. c. 235), an antipope who withstood three popes, was reconciled in exile and died for the faith. He is accredited with the Apostolic Constitutions, from which is derived a Eucharistic Prayer popularly used today.

Our faith does not rely on vain discussions, it does not yield to the impulse of feelings nor to the persuasions of eloquent persons, but it appeals to the words spoken by divine authority. These words God entrusted to his Word, and the Word gave utterance to them, to turn us back from disobedience, not constraining us by force, as a slave, but offering us the liberty of making a choice by our own free will.

This Word the Father sent at the end of time. . . . We know that he was made one of our nature, for if he had not been it would have been useless of him to command us to imitate him as our master. Indeed, if he had been constituted differently from me, how could he have ordained me to be like him, I who am feeble from birth? So that he might not be different from us, he bore exhaustion, he willed to be hungry and he did not refuse to be thirsty, he did not avoid sleep or reject suffering, he was obedient to death and was made manifest by his resurrection. In all this he was offering his humanity as first fruits, so that you in your suffering would not lose courage—you too, a man as he was, await what God has given him.

—*Saint Hippolytus*

AUGUST 4
St. John Vianney

St. John Vianney (1786–1859) seemed to be lacking in the ordinary gifts necessary to make a good priest, but his dedication and zeal made the holy Curé of Ars worthy to be the patron of parish priests.

We have a splendid function to fulfill: to pray and to love. You pray, you love: there you have our happiness on earth.

Prayer is nothing else than union with God. If you have a heart that is pure and united with God, you feel within yourself a balm, a sweetness that intoxicates, a light that dazzles. In this intimate union, God and you are like two pieces of wax melted into one; you can no longer be separated. It is a beautiful thing, this union of God with his little creatures. It is a happiness that goes beyond our understanding.

We had deserved not to pray, but God, in his goodness, allowed us to speak with him. Our prayer is an incense which he received with extreme pleasure.

My children, your heart is small, but prayer enlarges it and makes it capable of loving God. Prayer is a foretaste of heaven, a passing glimpse into paradise. It never leaves us without sweetness. It is a honey which comes down into the soul and sweetens everything. Sorrow melts away before a well-offered prayer, like snow before the sun.

Prayer makes time pass very swiftly, and so agreeably that we do not notice how long it has taken. Listen to this, now: when I was rushing about the Bresse region, at the time when poor parish priests were nearly all ill, I used to pray to God all along the road. I assure you that the time was never long enough.

How often do we come to church not knowing what we have come to do and what we want to ask! Yet when we go to see someone in his home, we know perfectly well why we have come. There are people who look as though they are saying to God: I'm going out to say a word or two to you in order to get rid of you. I often think that when we come to adore our Lord, we would obtain all that we wanted if we asked it of him with a really living faith and with a heart that was really pure.

—*St. John Vianney*

AUGUST 5
Dedication of
St. Mary Major

The basilica of St. Mary Major, one of the four major basilicas of Rome, commemorates the declaration made by the Council of Ephesus that Mary is in truth the Mother of God.

If the servant of Christ by his care and heartfelt tenderness bears his little children again and again until Christ is formed in them, how much more is this true of the very Mother of Christ? Paul begot his children by preaching the Word of Truth, through which they were born again; but Mary, in a manner far more holy and marvelous, by giving birth to the Word himself. I do indeed praise the ministry of preaching in Paul, but far more do I admire and venerate that mystery of generation in Mary.

—*Blessed Guerric of Igny*

AUGUST 6
The Holy Transfiguration

One of the great theophanies marking Jesus' life—not only did the Holy Trinity manifest themselves, but Jesus' mission was clearly confirmed.

Upon Tabor, Jesus revealed to his disciples a heavenly mystery. While living among them he had spoken of the kingdom and of his second coming to glory, but to banish from their hearts any possible doubt concerning the kingdom and to confirm their faith in what lay in the future, he gave them on Mount Tabor a wonderful vision of his glory, a foreshadowing of the kingdom of heaven. It was as if he said to them: "As time goes on you may be in danger of losing your faith. To save you from this I say to you now that 'some standing here' listening to me 'will not taste death until they have seen the Son of Man coming' in the glory of the Father." Moreover, in order to assure us that Christ could command such power when he wished, the evangelist continues, "Six days later, Jesus took with him Peter, James and John and led them up a high mountain where they were alone. There, before their eyes, he was transfigured. His face shown like the sun, and his clothes became as white as light. Then the disciples saw Moses and Elijah appear, and they were talking to Jesus."

These are the divine wonders we celebrate today. This is the saving revelation given us upon the mountain. This is the festival of Christ that has drawn us here. Let us retire from the world, stand aloof from the earth, rise above the body, detach ourselves from creatures and turn to the Creator, to whom Peter exclaimed, "Lord, it is good for us to be here." It is indeed good to be here, as you have said, Peter. It is good to be with Jesus and to remain here for ever. What greater happiness or higher honor could we have than to be with God, to be made like him and to live in his light?

—*St. Anastasius of Sinai*

AUGUST 7
St. Cajetan

St. Cajetan (1480–1547), first a lawyer, then a priest, founded the Congregations of the Clerks Regular at Rome.

Do not forget that all the saints cannot endear you to Christ as much as you can yourself. It is entirely up to you. If you want Christ to love you and help you, you must love him and always make an effort to please him. Do not waver in your purpose, because even if all the saints and every single creature should abandon you, he will always be near you, whatever your needs.

You know, of course, that we are pilgrims in this world, on a journey to our true home in heaven. The man who becomes proud loses his way and rushes to death. While living here we should strive to gain eternal life. Yet of ourselves we cannot achieve this since we have lost it through sin. But Jesus Christ has recovered it for us. For this reason we must always be grateful to him and love him. We must always obey him and as far as possible remain united with him.

—*St. Cajetan*

AUGUST 8
St. Dominic

St. Dominic (c. 1170–1221), a canon of Osma in Spain, founded the Order of Preachers (Dominicans) to carry forward his crusade of truth against the heretics of his time.

For many years I have exhorted you in vain, with gentleness, preaching, praying, and weeping. But according to the proverb of my country, "Where blessing can accomplish nothing, blows may prevail." Must blows prevail where gentleness and blessings have been powerless?

—*St. Dominic*

AUGUST 10
St. Lawrence

St. Lawrence (d. 258), one of the seven deacons of Rome, courageously suffered martyrdom with good humor.

Turn me over now. I am done on this side.

—*St. Lawrence*

AUGUST 11
St. Clare of Assisi

St. Clare of Assisi (1194–1253), drawn by St. Francis into the way of Lady Poverty, became the mother of the Poor Clares, contemplative sisters of the Friars Minor.

I pray you, O most gentle Jesus, having redeemed me by baptism from original sin, so now by your Precious Blood, which is offered and received throughout the world, deliver me from all evils, past present and to come.

By your most cruel death give me lively faith, a firm hope and perfect charity, so that I may love you with all my heart and all my soul and all my strength. Make me firm and steadfast in good works and grant me perseverance in your service so that I may be able to please you always.

—*St. Clare*

AUGUST 13
St. Maximus the Confessor

St. Maximus the Confessor (580–662), formerly secretary to the Emperor, because of his loyalty to orthodox faith and to the Pope, suffered at the Emperor's hands a harsh exile which led to his death. Maximus' theological and mystical writing profoundly influenced Western spirituality through Bernard of Clairvaux.

The lamp placed on the stand of which Scripture speaks, is our Lord Jesus Christ, true light of the Father, who lightens every person, coming into the world. In taking our flesh, he became and called himself "lamp," that is to say, Wisdom and Word of God according to his nature and he is proclaimed in God's church through godliness and through faith. Glorified and manifested among the nations by the example of his life and by fidelity to God's commandments, he shines for all those who are in the house, which means for all in this world. The Word of God himself says this: "Nor do men light a lamp and put it under a bushel, but on a stand, and it gives light to all in the house." He calls himself a lamp, for he is God by nature and became flesh in the wisdom of the dispensation of salvation.

It seems to me that the great David was thinking of this when he said, speaking of the Savior: "Thy word is a lamp unto my feet and a light to my path." Our God and Savior delivers us from the gloom of ignorance and evil. And that is why, in Scripture, he is called a "lamp." In dispelling, like a lamp, the darkness of ignorance and the shadows of sin, he alone became for everyone the way of salvation. Through discernment and strength he leads to the Father those who are willing to go with him, as though on a path of righteousness, along the way of the divine commandments.

As to the stand, it is holy Church. The shining Word of God rests

on her preaching, enlightening men of the whole world as dwellers in
his house, and filling their spirits with knowledge of God. The Word
has no desire to remain under a bushel; he wants to be put where he
can be clearly seen, on top of the Church. Had he remained under
the letter of the law, as though under a bushel, the Word would have
deprived all of eternal light. He would have been unable to give
spiritual sight, contemplation, to those seeking to detach themselves
from the lure of the senses which can create illusion and which are
quick to perceive only those transitory things inherent in matter. But
placed on the stand which is the Church, founded on worship in
spirit and truth, he enlightens all.

—*St. Maximus*

AUGUST 15
Feast of the Assumption of the Blessed Virgin Mary

*The dogma of the corporeal assumption of the Holy Mother of God
was defined by Pope Pius XII in 1950, attesting to the age-old belief
of the Christian peoples East and West.*

Today the holy and life-containing ark of the living God who con-
ceived the Creator of the world in her womb, comes to rest in the
temple of God that is not made with hands. David, her ancestor,
dances with all his might, while angel choirs make melody, archangels honor her, and virtues glorify her.

How could she, in whom was the true Life of all, ever taste of
death. Yet she obeyed the law ordained by him whom she bore, and,
as a daughter of the first Adam, submitted to the ancient sentence
(for her Son, who is life itself, did not refuse it but as the mother of

the living God it is right that she should be raised up to him. God sent the first created man out of Eden "lest he put forth his hand and take also of the tree of life and eat and live for ever." How, then, could she who had received within her the very Life itself, which has neither beginning nor end, not be alive for all eternity?

Formerly, the first parents of our mortal race, intoxicated by the wine of disobedience, with the heart's vision weighed down by the drunkenness of transgression, the eyes of the mind heavy with the weight of sin, had fallen into the sleep of death. The Lord had driven them out of the paradise of Eden. Now, how could paradise not receive her who had committed no sin and the heavens not joyfully open their gates to her who had brought into the world the child of obedience to God, the Father?

Since Christ, who is the Life and the Truth, said, "Where I am, there shall my servant be also." How indeed could his mother not share his dwelling place with him? Since the pure and holy body, which the divine Word had united to himself in her, had risen from the tomb on the third day, it was fitting that she also should be carried away from the tomb and be lifted up into a greater and more perfect dwelling place, "into heaven itself." She who had sheltered the divine Word in her breast was to be lodged in the dwelling place of her Son. As the Savior had said that he would dwell in the courts of his own Father, it was significant that the mother should dwell in those of her Son. "In the house of the Lord, in the courts of the house of our God." For if that is the abode of all those who rejoice, where else should the cause of the rejoicing dwell?

—*St. John Damascene*

AUGUST 16
St. Stephen of Hungary

St. Stephen of Hungary (975–1038), first King of Hungary, was baptized with his father when he was ten. He did much to establish the Church in his new kingdom.

Be merciful to all who are suffering violence, keeping always in your heart the example of the Lord who said, "I desire mercy and not sacrifice." Be patient with everyone, not only with the powerful but also with the weak. Finally, be strong lest prosperity lift you up too much or adversity cast you down. Be humble in this life, that God may raise you up in the next. Be truly moderate and do not punish or condemn anyone immoderately. Be gentle so that you may never oppose justice. Be honorable so that you may never voluntarily bring disgrace upon anyone. Be chaste so that you may avoid all the foulness of lust like the pangs of death.

All of these virtues I have noted make up the royal crown and without them no one is fit to rule here on earth or attain the heavenly kingdom.

—St. Stephen

AUGUST 19
St. John Eudes

St. John Eudes (1601–1680), an Oratorian, founded the Congregation of Jesus and Mary. He is noted for promoting devotion to the Sacred Heart of Jesus.

Our loving Savior in various places in the Scriptures, assures us that he is ever watchful for us, that we are and always will be in his most compassionate care. How he carries us in his heart he is not content with telling us once or twice but in one place he even repeats it five times in succession (Isaiah 46:3–4). Elsewhere he tells us the same thing in many ways. Although, he says, it may sometimes happen that a mother can forget her child, yet he will never forget us, and he has engraved us on his hands to have us ever before him. Who ever touches one of us, he says, touches the apple of his eye. Again, we should not be anxious about how we are going to get enough to eat or wear, because he well knows our needs and takes care of them. He has even counted the very hairs on our heads and not one shall perish. He also tells us that as he loves his Father so this Father loves us and that his own love for us is the same as his Father's love for him. He wishes us to be where he is, that is, he wishes us to dwell with him in his Father's heart.

—St. John Eudes

AUGUST 20
St. Bernard of Clairvaux

St. Bernard of Clairvaux (1090–1153) was truly the spiritual father of all Christendom in the first half of the twelfth century. He became a monk at twenty-three and founded some sixty monasteries, wrote many powerful sermons and treatises, and guided popes and kings, bishops and common folk.

For my part, I find delight and consolation in the very thought of Saint Benedict, although I can never pronounce this blessed father's name without a feeling of confusion. Let me explain the reason. Following his example, I, with you, have renounced the world and embraced the monastic life; but I have also in common with him the title of abbot, in which you do not share. Benedict was an abbot and I too am an abbot. But oh, what an abbot he was and what an abbot am I! The title is the same in both, but in one it is only "the shadow of a great name." The ministry also is the same, but alas for me, how different are the ministers! how different the administrations! Woe is me! O blessed Benedict, if in the world to come I shall be as far removed from you as I find myself distant now from the model of your holiness! But it is not necessary for me to dwell upon this point in addressing you, my brothers, who, as I cannot doubt, know me perfectly. I only ask you to lighten with your brotherly compassion my heavy burden of shame and fear.

—*St. Bernard*

AUGUST 22
The Queenship of the Blessed Virgin Mary

Mother of the King, according to the traditions of her people, the Queen Mother holds an especially honored and powerful place in the Kingdom of her Son.

Because of the honor due her Son, it was indeed fitting for the Virgin Mother to have first ruled upon earth and then be raised up to heaven in glory. It was fitting that her fame be spread in this world below, so that she might enter the heights of heaven in overwhelming blessedness. Just as she was borne from virtue to virtue by the spirit of the Lord, so she was transported from earthly renown to heavenly brightness.

The virgin John, rejoicing that the Virgin Mother was entrusted to him at the cross, cared for her with the other apostles here below. The angels rejoiced to see their queen, the apostles rejoiced to see their lady, and both obeyed her with loving devotion.

Able to preserve both flesh and spirit from death she bestowed health-giving salve on bodies and souls. Has anyone ever come away from her troubled or saddened or ignorant of the heavenly mysteries? Who has not returned to everyday life gladdened and joyful because his request had been granted by the Mother of God?

—St. Amadeus of Lausanne

AUGUST 23
St. Rose of Lima

St. Rose of Lima (1586–1617), joined the Third Order of St. Dominic, wore the habit, and lived a life of great austerity in her parental home.

Our Lord and Savior lifted up his voice and said with incomparable majesty: "Let all know that grace comes after tribulation. Let them know that without the burden of affliction it is impossible to reach the height of grace. Let them know that the gifts of grace increase as the struggles increase. Let all take care not to stray and be deceived. This is the only true stairway to paradise and without the cross they can find no road to climb to heaven."

When I heard these words, a strong force came upon me and seemed to place me in the middle of a street, so that I might say in a loud voice to people of every age, sex and status: "Hear, O people, hear, O nations. I am warning you about the commandment of Christ by using words that came from his own lips: We cannot obtain grace unless we suffer affliction. We must heap trouble upon trouble to attain a deep participation in the divine nature, the glory of the children of God and perfect happiness."

If only mortals would learn how great it is to possess divine grace, how beautiful, how noble, how precious. How many riches it hides within itself, how many joys and delights!

—St. Rose

AUGUST 25
King St. Louis IX

St. Louis IX (1214–1270), father of eleven children, died while crusading to regain the tomb of Christ.

My dearest son, my first instruction is that you should love the Lord your God with all your heart and all your strength. Without this there is no salvation. Keep yourself, my son, from everything that you know displeases God, that is to say, from every mortal sin. You should permit yourself to be tormented by every kind of martyrdom before you would allow yourself to commit a mortal sin. If the Lord has permitted you to have some trial, bear it willingly and with gratitude, considering that it has happened for your good and that perhaps you well deserve it. If the Lord bestows upon you any kind of prosperity, thank him humbly and see that you become no worse for it either through vain pride or anything else, because you ought not to oppose God or offend him in the matter of his gifts.

Be kindhearted to the poor, the unfortunate and the afflicted. Give them as much help and consolation as you can. Thank God for all the benefits he has bestowed upon you, that you may be worthy to receive greater. Always side with the poor rather than with the rich until you are certain of the truth.

Be devout and obedient to your mother the Church of Rome and the supreme Pontiff as your spiritual father.

—St. Louis

AUGUST 27
St. Monica

St. Monica (331–387), the mother of St. Augustine, won his conversion by her tears and prayers.

My mother said: "Son, as far as I am concerned, nothing in this life now gives me any pleasure. I do not know why I am still here, since I have no further hopes in this world. I did have one reason for wanting to live a little longer: to see you become a Catholic Christian before I died. God has lavished his gifts on me in that respect, for I know that you have even renounced earthly happiness to be his servant. So what am I doing here?"

Thereupon she said: "Bury my body wherever you will; let not care of it cause you any concern. One thing only I ask of you, that you remember me at the altar of the Lord wherever you may be."

—*St. Augustine*

AUGUST 28
St. Augustine

St. Augustine (354–430), was one of the greatest theologians of the patristic period. Baptized at thirty-three, he became bishop of Hippo in Africa only eight years later and served there until his death.

My love of you, O Lord, is not some vague feeling: it is positive and certain. Your word struck into my heart and from that moment I loved you. Besides this, all about me, heaven and earth and all that they contain proclaim that I should love you. . . .

But what do I love when I love you? Not material beauty or beauty of a temporal order; not the brilliance of earthly light, so welcome to our eyes; not the sweet melody of harmony and song; not the fragrance of flowers, perfumes, and spices; not manna or honey; not limbs such as the body delights to embrace. It is not these that I love when I love my God. And yet, when I love him, it is true that I love a light of a certain kind that I love in my inner self, when my soul is bathed in light that is not bound by space; when it listens to sound that never dies away; when it breathes fragrance that is not borne away on the wind; when it tastes food that is never consumed by the eating; when it clings to an embrace from which it is not severed by fulfillment of desire. This is what I love when I love my God.

—St. Augustine

AUGUST 29
St. John the Baptist

St. John the Baptist, cousin of Our Lord, was beheaded for his steadfast witness to truth and righteousness.

There is no doubt that blessed John suffered imprisonment and chains as a witness to our Redeemer, whose forerunner he was, and gave his life for him. His persecutor had demanded not that he should deny Christ, but only that he should keep silent about the truth. Nevertheless, he died for Christ. Does Christ not say: "I am the truth"? Therefore, because John shed his blood for the truth, he surely died for Christ.

In his birth, preaching and baptizing, he bore witness to the coming birth, preaching and baptism of Christ, and by his own suffering he showed that Christ also would suffer.

Such was the quality and strength of the man who accepted the end of this present life by shedding his blood after the long imprisonment. He preached the freedom of heavenly peace yet was thrown into irons by unholy men. He was locked away in the darkness of prison, though he came bearing witness to the Light of life and deserved to be called a bright and shining lamp by that Light himself, who is Christ.

—St. Bede the Venerable

SEPTEMBER

September 3
St. Gregory the Great

St. Gregory the Great (540–604), a monk and disciple of Benedict of Nursia, was elected pope in 590. He is best known for sending St. Augustine to evangelize Britain and for his pastoral writings, including the life of St. Benedict.

As the earth has produced us all, it is not without reason that we call her our mother. As it is written: "A heavy yoke is upon the sons of Adam, from the day they came forth from their mother's womb till the day they return to the mother of all." Blessed Job, then, that he might mourn patiently for all that he had lost in this world, pays attentive heed to the condition in which he entered it; and, in order to conserve this patience he thinks still further of how he will leave it: "Naked I came from my mother's womb and naked shall I return." That is to say, naked did the earth bare me when I came into the world, naked will the earth receive me again when I depart. I have lost what I should have to give up after receiving it: have I lost anything that was really mine?

Since comfort is to be derived not only from the consideration of our creation but also from the justice of the Creator, he adds, "The Lord has given, the Lord has taken away; as it pleased the Lord, so has he done." The holy man, under trial from the adversary, has lost everything, yet knowing that satan has no power against him to tempt him save by the Lord's permission, he does not say, "The Lord gave and Satan has taken away," but "The Lord gave, the Lord has taken away." It would be a thing to grieve for, did the enemy take away what the Lord has given, but since he who takes away is no other than he who gave, the Giver has only taken away his own and has not taken anything of ours. For if we have from him all that we make use of in our present life, why should we complain if he thinks good to take back that which in his goodness he had lent?

Now let us hear how in the end Job extols his Judge with blessing: "Blessed be the name of the Lord." He finally blesses the Lord for all that he felt to be right. This man under the scourge of affliction, utters a song of praise to the Lord.

—*St. Gregory*

SEPTEMBER 7
Blessed William
of St. Thierry

Blessed William of St. Thierry (c. 1085–1148) was an intimate friend and disciple of St. Bernard of Clairvaux. After serving as abbot of St. Thierry and leading the Benedictines to reform, he retired to the Cistercian abbey of Signy. He has left us very rich teaching on the spiritual life and prayer, developing a deep Trinitarian mysticism.

You alone, my God, are truly Lord, you who in ruling us, save us, while for us, to serve you is nothing else but to receive from you salvation. How, then, are we in fact saved by you, Lord, to whom deliverance belongs and whose blessing is upon your people if it is not by receiving from you the gifts of loving you and receiving your love? And to that end, Lord, you willed that the Son of your right hand, he whom you made one with yourself, should be called Jesus— Savior. It is he who will save his people from their sins. There is salvation in no one else. It is he who taught us to love him, when he first loved us, even to death on the cross. By loving and choosing us for himself, he awakens in us love for him who first loved us to the uttermost.

—*Blessed William*

SEPTEMBER 8
The Nativity of the Blessed Virgin Mary

Because of her immaculate conception, the birth of Mary was a wholly beautiful event, to be celebrated in view of what it promised for all.

The radiant and manifest coming of God to men most certainly needed a joyful prelude to introduce the great gift of salvation to us. The present festival, the birth of the Mother of God, is the prelude while the final act is the foreordained union of the Word with flesh. Today, the Virgin is born, tended and formed, and prepared for her role as Mother of God, who is the universal King of the ages.

Justly then do we celebrate this mystery since it signifies to us a double grace. We are led toward the truth, and we are led away from our condition of slavery to the letter of the law. How can this be? Darkness yields before the coming light, and grace exchanges legalism for freedom.

Therefore, let all creation sing and dance and unite to make worthy contribution to the celebration of this day. Let there be one common festival for saints in heaven and those on earth. Let everything, mundane things and those above, join in festive celebration. Today this created world is raised to the dignity of a holy place for him who made all things. The creature is newly prepared to be a divine dwelling place for the Creator.

—*St. Andrew of Crete*

SEPTEMBER 9
St. Peter Claver

*St. Peter Claver (1580–1654) joined the Jesuits when he was twenty-
two and went to the missions in Colombia. There, working among
the slaves, he lived out a vow to be "the slave of the blacks forever."*

Yesterday, May 30, 1627, on the feast of the Most Holy Trinity,
numerous blacks, brought from the rivers of Africa, disembarked
from a large ship. Carrying two baskets of oranges, lemons, sweet
biscuits, and I know not what else, we hurried toward them. We had
to force our way through the crowd until we reached the sick. Large
numbers of the sick were lying on the wet ground or rather in pud-
dles of mud. To prevent excessive dampness, someone had thought to
build up a mound with a mixture of tiles and broken pieces of bricks.
This, then, was their couch, a very uncomfortable one not only for
that reason but especially because they were naked, without any
clothing to protect them.

We laid aside our cloaks and brought from a warehouse whatever
was handy to build a platform. In that way we covered a space to
which we transferred the sick by forcing a passage through bands of
slaves. Then we divided the sick into two groups: one group my
companion approached with an interpreter, while I addressed the
other group. There were two blacks, nearer death than life, already
cold, whose pulse could scarcely be detected. With the help of a tile
we pulled some live coals together and placed them in the middle
near the dying men. Into this fire we tossed aromatics. Then, using
our own cloaks, for they had nothing of the sort, and to ask the
owners for others would have been a waste of words, we provided for
them a smoke treatment, by which they seemed to recover their
warmth and the breath of life. The joy in their eyes as they looked at

us was something to see. This is how we talked to them, not with words but with our hands and our actions.

After this we began an elementary instruction about baptism, that is, the wonderful effects of the sacrament on body and soul. When by their answers to our questions they showed they had sufficiently understood this, we went on to a more extensive instruction, namely, about the one God, who rewards and punishes each one according to his merit, and the rest. Finally when they appeared sufficiently prepared, we told them the mysteries of the Trinity, the Incarnation and the Passion. Showing them Christ fastened to the cross, as he is depicted on the baptismal font on which streams of blood flow down from his wounds, we led them in reciting an act of contrition in their own language.

—*St. Peter*

SEPTEMBER 12
Feast of the Holy Name of Mary

Christian piety has always held the name of the Mother of God in special reverence.

"And the Virgin's name was Mary." Let us now say a few words about this name, which means "star of the sea" and is so becoming the Virgin Mother. Surely she is very fittingly likened to a star. . . . O you, whoever you are, who feel in the tidal wave of this world you are nearer to being tossed about among the squalls and gales than treading on dry land, if you do not want to founder in the tempest, do not avert your eyes from the brightness of this star. When the wind of temptation blows up within you, when you strike upon the rock of tribulation, gaze up at this star, call out to Mary. Whether you are being tossed about by the waves of pride or ambition or slander or jealousy, gaze up at this star, call out to Mary. When rage or greed or fleshly desires are battering the skiff of your soul, gaze up at Mary. When the immensity of your sins weighs you down and you are bewildered by the loathsomeness of your conscience when the terrifying thought of judgement appalls you and you begin to founder in the gulf of sadness and despair, think of Mary. In dangers, in hardships, in every doubt, think of Mary, call out to Mary. Keep her in your mouth, keep her in your heart. Follow the example of her life and you will obtain the favor of her prayer. Following her you will never go astray. Asking her help, you will never despair. Keeping her in your thoughts, you will never wander away. With your hand in hers, you will never stumble. With her protecting you, you will not be afraid. With her leading you, you will never tire. Her kindness will see you through to the end. Then you will know from your own experience how true it is that "the Virgin's name was Mary."

—*St. Bernard of Clairvaux*

SEPTEMBER 13
St. John Chrysostom

St. John Chrysostom (c. 344–407) was a man of great eloquence. In 398 he was elected archbishop of Constantinople. His efforts at reform caused him to suffer much and die in exile.

Nothing is more frigid than a Christian who does not care about the salvation of others. You cannot plead the excuse of poverty here; the widow who gave her two mites will stand to accuse you. Peter said, "Silver or gold I have none." Paul was so poor he often went hungry, lacking necessary food. You cannot plead lowliness. They were of low estate and so were their parents. You cannot allege lack of education or preparation. They were unlearned men. You cannot plead infirmity. Timothy was often laid low by sickness and the Apostle had to counsel him to take a little wine for his stomach. Every one can profit his neighbor if he will do what he can.

Do not say, It is impossible for me to lead others to the faith. If you are a Christian, it is impossible for it not to be so. The natural properties of things cannot be denied. This witnessing to others is part of the very nature of being a Christian. It would be easier for the sun to cease to shine and give forth heat than for a Christian not to send forth light; easier for the light to be darkness than for this to be so.

—St. John

SEPTEMBER 14
Triumph of the Holy Cross

This feast commemorates the dedication in 335 of the basilica over the site of Calvary wherein was enshrined the relics of the true cross found by St. Helena.

We are celebrating the feast of the cross which drove away darkness and brought in the light. As we keep this feast, we are lifted up with the crucified Christ, leaving behind us earth and sin so that we may gain the things above. So great and outstanding a possession is the cross that he who wins it has won a treasure. Rightly could I call this treasure the fairest of all fair things and the costliest, in fact as well as in name, for on it and through it and for its sake the riches of salvation that had been lost were restored to us.

Therefore, the cross is something wonderfully great and honorable. It is great because through the cross the many noble acts of Christ found their consummation—very many indeed, for both his miracles and his suffering were fully rewarded with victory. The cross is honorable because it is both the sign of God's suffering and the trophy of his victory. It stands for his suffering because on it he freely suffered unto death. But it is also his trophy because it was the means by which the devil was wounded and death conquered; the bared gates of hell were smashed and the cross became the one common salvation of the whole world. If you would understand that the cross is Christ's triumph, hear what he himself said, "When I am lifted up, then I will draw all to myself."

—St. Andrew of Crete

SEPTEMBER 15
Our Lady of Sorrows

At the presentation of Jesus in the Temple, Simeon prophesied how much Mary would suffer as her Son carried out his redemptive mission. This we ponder today.

The martyrdom of the Virgin is set forth in the prophecy of Simeon and in the actual story of our Lord's passion. The holy old man said of the infant Jesus, "He had been established as a sign which will be contradicted." He went on to say to Mary, "And your own heart will be pierced by a sword."

Truly, O blessed Mother, a sword has pierced your heart. For only by passing through your heart could the sword enter the flesh of your Son. Indeed, after your Jesus—who belongs to everyone, but is especially yours—gave up his life, the cruel spear, which was not withheld from his lifeless body, tore open his side. Clearly it did not touch his soul and could not harm him, but it did pierce your heart. Thus the violence of sorrow has cut through your heart. We rightly call you martyr, since the effect of compassion in you has gone beyond the endurance of physical suffering.

Do not be surprised, brothers, that Mary is said to be a martyr in spirit. Let him be surprised who does not remember the words of Paul, that one of the greatest crimes of the Gentiles was that they were without love. That was far from the heart of Mary; let it be far from her servants.

She died in spirit through a love unlike any other since his.

—*St. Bernard of Clairvaux*

SEPTEMBER 16
St. Cyprian

St. Cyprian (c. 200–258), a pagan scholar who became a Christian scholar, was elected bishop of Carthage in northern Africa. After seven difficult and often stormy years, he was beheaded for Christ.

The Master of peace and unity would not have all pray singly and severally, since when anyone prays he is not to pray only for himself. For we neither say "My Father, who art in heaven" or "Give me this day my bread" nor does each individual pray for his own debt to be forgiven, nor does he ask that he himself alone should not be led into temptation, nor that he only should be delivered from evil. Our prayer is general and for all; and when we pray, we pray not for one person but for all, because we are all one. God, the master of peace and concord, so willed that one should pray for all even as he himself bore us all. The three children in the fiery furnace kept this rule of prayer, being in unison in prayer and agreeing in spirit. The authority of the Scriptures tells us this, and in teaching how they pray it gives an example which we ought to imitate in our prayers, so that we may become like them. "The three," it says, "as out of one mouth sang a hymn and blessed the Lord." They spoke as though out of one mouth, although Christ had not yet taught them to pray. Hence their words in prayer were effectual, because the Lord was gained by the simple, peaceful, and spiritual praying. We find, too, that the Apostles prayed in this way after the Lord's ascension. "All these," we are told, "with one accord devoted themselves to prayer."

—St. Cyprian

SEPTEMBER 17
St. Robert Bellarmine

St. Robert Bellarmine (1542–1621) entered the Jesuits at eighteen and distinguished himself as a student, professor, and rector of the Roman College. He served as archbishop of Capua as well as a cardinal at Rome.

What command, Lord, do you give your servants? "Take my yoke upon you," you say. And what is this yoke of yours like? "My yoke," you say, "is easy and my burden light." Who would not be glad to bear a yoke that does not press hard but caresses? Who would not be glad for a burden that does not weigh heavy but refreshes? And so you were right to add: "And you will find rest for your souls." And what is this yoke of yours that does not weary, but gives rest? It is, of course, that first and greatest commandment: "You shall love the Lord your God with all your heart." What is easier, sweeter, more pleasant, than to love goodness, beauty and love, the fullness of which you are, O Lord, my God?

Is it not true that you promised those who keep your commandments a reward more desirable than great wealth and sweeter than honey? You promise a most abundant reward, for as your apostle James says, "The Lord has prepared a crown of life for those who love him." What is this crown of life? It is surely a greater good than we can conceive of or desire, as Saint Paul says, quoting Isaiah, "Eye has not seen, ear has not heard, nor has it so much as dawned on the human person what God has prepared for those who love him."

—*St. Robert*

SEPTEMBER 21
St. Matthew

*St. Matthew, or Levi, was working as a tax collector in Capernaum
when Jesus called him to be his follower. He wrote the first Gospel
and is said to have preached in the East and died a martyr's death.*

Jesus noticed a tax collector, Levi by name, sitting by the customs
house, and said to him, "Follow me." And leaving everything he got
up and followed Jesus.

In Jesus' honor Levi held a great reception in his house, and with
them at table was a large gathering of tax collectors and others. The
Pharisees and their scribes complained to Jesus' disciples and said,
"Why do you eat and drink with tax collectors and sinners?" Jesus
said to them in reply, "It is not those who are well who need the
doctor, but the sick. I have not come to call the virtuous, but sinners
to repentance."

—St. Luke

SEPTEMBER 27
St. Vincent de Paul

*A slave who became chaplain to the galley slaves, a court chaplain
who preferred to go serve the poor, St. Vincent de Paul (c. 1580–
1660) founded the Congregation of the Mission and, with Louise de
Marillac, the Daughters of Charity. He also inspired the founding of
parochial societies to help the poor.*

It is our duty to prefer service to the poor to everything else and to
offer such service as quickly as possible. If a needy person requires
medicine or other help during prayer time, do whatever has to be
done with peace of mind. Offer the deed to God as your prayer.

Do not become upset or feel guilty because you interrupted prayer
to serve the poor. God is not neglected if you leave him for such
service. One of God's works is merely interrupted so that another
can be carried out. Charity is certainly greater than any rule.

—St. Vincent

SEPTEMBER 29
Archangels Michael, Gabriel, and Raphael

These particular archangels are known by name because of the accounts of their missions in the Sacred Scriptures.

You should be aware that the word "angel" denotes a function rather than a nature. Those holy spirits of heaven have indeed always been spirits. They can only be called angels when they deliver some message. Moreover, those who deliver messages of lesser importance are called "angels" and those who proclaim messages of supreme importance are called "archangels."

And so it was that not merely an angel but the Archangel Gabriel was sent to the Virgin Mary. It was only fitting that the highest angel should come to announce the greatest of all messages.

Some angels are given proper names to denote the service they are empowered to perform. Personal names are assigned to some, not because they could not be known without them but rather to denote their ministry when they come among us. Thus, Michael means "Who is like God?"; Gabriel is "The Strength of God"; and Raphael is "God's Remedy."

Whenever some act of wondrous power must be performed, Michael is sent, so that his action and his name may make it clear that no one can do what God does by his superior power.

So too Gabriel, who is called God's strength, was sent to Mary. He came to announce the One who appeared as a humble man to quell the cosmic powers. Thus God's strength announced the coming of the Lord of the heavenly powers, mighty in battle.

Raphael means, as I have said, God's remedy, for when he touched Tobit's eyes in order to cure him, he banished the darkness of his blindness. Thus, since he is to heal, he is rightly called God's remedy.

—St. Gregory the Great

SEPTEMBER 30
St. Jerome

St. Jerome (c. 342–420), monk and ascetic, superior of a monastery in Bethlehem, was one of the great Scripture scholars of his time, producing a Latin translation of the Bible and many commentaries.

What is that promised land that the Jews obtained upon their return from Egypt, seeing that their ancestors had already possessed it before them and that it was therefore no longer promised but restored to them? Most of us have asked this question and believe that we must look for another promised land, the one of which David said, in a psalm: "I believe that I shall see the goodness of the Lord in the land of the living." And our Lord said in the Gospel, "Blessed are the meek, for they shall inherit the earth." David, when he sang these inspired words, was indeed living in the promised land, and not only did he dwell in the land of Judea, but he had conquered many nations in a region which extended from the Torrent of Egypt to the river Euphrates. How then could he believe that he was going to receive what he already possessed through victory? And in order not to leave his Jewish readers in the slightest doubt as to the nature of this land that he longed to see, he indicates it in so many words when he says, "I believe that I shall see the goodness of the Lord in the land of the living." The land of Judah, was not the land of the living.

The land of the living, it is the land in which the goodness of the Lord has been prepared for the saints and the meek. Before our Lord and Savior came in the flesh, this goodness was inaccessible, even to Abraham. The land of the living, the land of riches and of the goodness of God, the first Adam had lost it and the second Adam found it again, or rather, the first had lost it and the second has restored it.

—*St. Jerome*

OCTOBER

OCTOBER 1
St. Therese of Lisieux

St. Therese of Lisieux (1873–1897) entered Carmel at the age of sixteen and in seven short years attained very great holiness through much suffering. Her autobiography became very popular.

My little life is to suffer, and that's it! Otherwise, I wouldn't be able to say, My God, this is for the Church, this is for France, etc. God knows best what to do with these sufferings; I've given them all to him to do with as he pleases. Besides, it would tire me out to tell him, Give this to Peter, that to Paul. When a Sister asks me for anything, I do it right away and then give it no further thought. When I pray for my brother missionaries, I don't offer my sufferings. I say simply, My God, give them everything I desire for myself.

—*St. Therese*

OCTOBER 2
Guardian Angels

Catholic tradition holds that each person has been blessed with the particular care of one of the angels, a special guardian for the journey through life.

"He has given his angels charge over you to guard you in all your ways. Let them thank the Lord for his mercy, his wonderful works are for the children of men." Let them give thanks and say among the nations, the Lord has done great things for them. Lord, who are we that you have made yourself known to us, or why do you incline your heart to us? As you incline your heart to us, you show us your care and your concern. You send your only Son and the grace of your Spirit, and promise us a vision of your countenance. And so that nothing in heaven should be wanting in your concern for us, you send those blessed spirits to serve us, assigning them as our guardians and our teachers.

"He has given his angels charge over you to guard you in all your ways." These words should fill you with respect, inspire devotion and instill confidence; respect for the presence of angels, devotion because of their loving service, and confidence because of their protection. And so the angels are here; they are at your side, they are with you, present on your behalf. They are here to protect you and to serve you. But even if it is God who has given them this charge, we must nevertheless be grateful to them for the great love with which they obey and come to help us in our great need.

So let us be devoted and grateful to such great protectors. Let us return their love and honor them as we can and should. Yet all our love and honor must be to him, for it is from him that they receive all that makes them worthy of our love and respect.

We should then, my brothers, show our affection for the angels. For one day they will be our coheirs just as here below they are our guardians and trustees appointed and set over us by the Father. We are God's children although it does not seem so, because we are still but small children under guardians and trustees.

Even though we are children and have a long, a very long and dangerous way to go, with such protectors what have we to fear? They who keep us in all our ways cannot be overpowered or led astray, much less lead us astray. They are loyal, prudent, powerful. Why then are we afraid? We have only to follow them, stay close to them, and we shall dwell under the protection of God's heaven.

—St. Bernard of Clairvaux

OCTOBER 4
St. Francis of Assisi

St. Francis of Assisi (1181–1226), one of the most popular saints in the calendar, followed the way of absolute poverty and drew hundreds to follow him, founding the Friars Minor and, with Saint Clare, the Poor Clares. He bore the wounds of Our Lord in his own body.

Brother Leo, although the Friars Minor in every land set a great example of holiness and of good edification, nevertheless, write and note diligently that therein is not perfect joy. . . .

When we arrive at Saint Mary of the Angels, soaked with rain, frozen with cold, and befouled with mud, and afflicted with hunger, and shall knock at the door and the doorkeeper shall say angrily, "Who are you?" and we shall say, "We are two of your friars," and he shall say, "You are not telling the truth, but you are two base fellows who go about deceiving the world and robbing the alms of the poor, go away;" and instead of letting us in he will make us stay outside in the snow and rain, cold and hungry, even until night; then if we shall bear such great wrong and such cruelty and such rebuffs patiently, without disquieting ourselves and without murmuring against him; and shall think humbly and charitably that the door-keeper really believes us to be that which he has called us, and that God makes him speak against us; O Brother Leo, write that here is perfect joy.

And if we persevere in knocking and he shall come forth enraged and drive us away with insults and blows as importunate rascals, saying, "Go away, vilest of petty thieves, go to the hospice. You shall neither eat nor lodge here." If we shall bear this patiently and with joy and love, O Brother Leo, write that herein is perfect joy.

And if, constrained by hunger and cold and the night, we continue to knock and shall call and beseech for the love of God, with great weeping, that he open to us and let us in, and he, greatly offended, shall say, "These are importunate rascals; I will pay them as they deserve," and shall come forth with a knotty club and take us by the cowl and throw us to the ground and roll us in the snow and beat us pitilessly with that club; if we shall bear all these things patiently and with cheerfulness, thinking on the suffering of Christ the blessed, the which we ought to bear patiently for his love; O Brother Leo, write that here and in this is perfect joy.

Therefore hear the conclusion, Brother Leo. Above all the gifts and graces of the Holy Spirit which Christ grants to his friends, is that of self-conquest and of willingly bearing sufferings, injuries and reproaches and discomforts for the love of Christ; because in all the other gifts of God we cannot glory, inasmuch as they are not ours, but of God. As the Apostle says, "What have you that you did not receive? If then you received it, why do you boast as if it were not a gift?" But in the cross of tribulation and affliction we may glory, because this is our own; and therefore the Apostle says: "Far be it from me to glory except in the cross of our Lord Jesus Christ."

—St. Francis

OCTOBER 6
St. Bruno

St. Bruno (1035–1101), at the age of fifty, left his post as professor of theology at Cologne and with six companions established the first Charterhouse.

I live in a desert in Calabria, far from the dwellings of others. I have with me my brethren in religion, some of whom are filled with wisdom. They keep watch in holiness and endurance.

There is a benefit and a joy which comes from the solitude and silence of the desert to those who love them, and only those who experience them understand this. Here, strong men can get all the recollection they desire and live an inner life, growing in virtue, feeding on the fruits of paradise. Here one can come to that serene vision and purity of heart that can see God. Here we have a busy ease and a quiet activity. Here God gives his athletes the reward they desire, a peace unknown to the world and joy in the Holy Spirit. This is that better part that Mary has chosen and that shall never be taken from her.

How I wish, dear brothers and sisters, that you were on fire with love for God. If that love were firmly fixed in your heart, how quickly the glory of the world, which is so clinging and alluring, would seem to you wretched. You would easily reject the riches whose care weighs down your soul. For what is more unnatural, unreasonable, and unjust than to prefer the creature to the Creator, to follow transient goods instead of those which are eternal, to prefer earth to heaven?

—*St. Bruno*

OCTOBER 9
St. John Leonardi

St. John Leonardi (1541–1609), a pharmacist who became a priest, founded the Order of Clerics Regular of the Mother of God. He was also instrumental in the creation of the Society for the Propagation of the Faith.

Those who want to work for moral reform in the world must seek the glory of God before all else. Because he is the source of all good, they must wait for his help, and pray for it in this difficult and necessary undertaking. They must then present themselves to those they seek to reform, as mirrors of every virtue and as lamps on a lampstand. Their upright lives and noble conduct must shine before all who are in the house of God. In this way they will gently entice the members of the Church to reform, lest, in the words of the Council of Trent, they demand of the body what is not found in the head, and thus upset the whole order of the Lord's household.

They will be like skilled physicians taking pains to dispose of all the diseases that afflict the Church and require a cure. They will ready themselves to provide suitable remedies for each illness.

—*St. John*

OCTOBER 13
Our Lady of Fatima

In 1917 the Blessed Virgin Mary appeared on numerous occasions to three poor shepherd children near the town of Fatima, Portugal, urging prayer and penance and confirming her visits with a great prodigy.

Make everything you do a sacrifice and offer it as an act of reparation for sins by which God is offended and in supplication for the conversion of sinners. Bring peace to your country in this way. . . . Above all, accept and bear in submission the sufferings sent you by our Lord.

—*Our Lady of Fatima*

OCTOBER 15
St. Teresa of Jesus

St. Teresa of Jesus (1515–1582), often called St. Teresa of Avila, reformed the Carmelite Order and wrote practical books on prayer which won for her the title of Doctor of the Church.

O Lord! All our ills come from not fixing our eyes on you. If we looked at nothing else but the way, we should soon arrive, but we fall a thousand times and stumble and go astray because we do not keep our eyes fixed on the true Way.

In seems as though we were not Christians at all, nor had ever in our lives read the Passion. Some slight disrespect is shown us and we at once cry out, "We are not saints!" So I say, God deliver us from saying, "We are not saints" when we fall into any imperfection. Let there be nothing which we know would further our Lord's service that we dare not undertake with the assistance of his grace.

God aids the valiant and is no respecter of persons. Both to you and to me he will give the help needed.

—St. Teresa

OCTOBER 16
St. Margaret Mary Alacoque

St. Margaret Mary Alacoque (1647–1690), a Visitation nun at Paray-le-Monial, enjoyed many visions of our Lord in which he revealed to her the immense love burning in his sacred heart.

The sacred heart of Christ is an inexhaustible fountain and its sole desire is to pour itself out into the hearts of the humble so as to free them and prepare them to lead lives according to his good pleasure.

From this divine heart three streams flow endlessly. The first is the stream of mercy for sinners; it pours into their hearts sentiments of contrition and repentance. The second is the stream of charity which helps all in need and especially aids those seeking perfection in order to find means of surmounting their difficulties. From the third stream flows love and light for the benefit of his friends who have attained perfection; these he wishes to unite to himself so that they may share his knowledge and commandments and, in their individual ways, devote themselves wholly to advancing his glory.

The divine heart is an abyss filled with all blessings and into it the poor should submerge all their needs. It is an abyss of joy in which all of us can immerse our sorrows. It is an abyss of lowliness to counteract our foolishness, and abyss of mercy for the wretched, an abyss of love to meet our every need.

—*St. Margaret Mary*

OCTOBER 17
St. Ignatius of Antioch

According to tradition St. Ignatius of Antioch (d. c. 107) was a disciple of St. John and was consecrated bishop of Antioch by St. Peter. He was taken to Rome to die for Christ. He has left us seven beautiful letters.

Let me be the food of beasts that I may come to God. I am his wheat, and I shall be ground by the teeth of beasts, that I may become Christ's pure bread. . . .

The fire, the cross, packs of wild beasts, lacerations, rendings, wrenching of bones, mingling of limbs, crunching of the whole body, the horrible tortures of the devil—let all these things come upon me, if only I may gain Jesus Christ.

—*St. Ignatius*

OCTOBER 18
St. Luke

St. Luke, a Gentile, was converted by St. Paul, served with him on his missionary journeys, and wrote the Acts of the Apostles as well as one of the Gospels.

In my earlier work, Theophilus, I dealt with everything Jesus had done and taught from the beginning until the day he gave his instructions to the apostles he had chosen through the Holy Spirit, and was taken up to heaven. He had shown himself alive to them after his Passion by many demonstrations for forty days. He had continued to appear to them and tell them about the kingdom of God. When he had been at table with them, he had told them not to leave Jerusalem, but to wait there for what the Father had promised. "It is," he had said, "what you have heard me speak about: John baptized with water but you, not many days from now, will be baptized with the Holy Spirit."

Now having met together, they asked him, "Lord, has the time come? Are you going to restore the kingdom of Israel?" He replied, "It is not for you to know the time or dates that the Father has decided by his own authority, but you will receive power when the Holy Spirit comes on you, and then you will be my witnesses not only in Jerusalem but through out Judea and Samaria and indeed to the ends of the earth."

As he said this he was lifted up while they looked on, and a cloud took him from their sight.

—St. Luke

OCTOBER 19

St. Isaac Jogues and St. John de Brebeuf

*St. Isaac Jogues (1606–1646) and St. John de Brebeuf (1593–1649)
were among the eight Jesuits who were martyred most savagely by
the American Indians.*

For two days now I have experienced a great desire to be a martyr
and to endure all the torments the martyrs suffered.

Jesus, my Lord and Savior, what can I give you in return for all
the favors you have conferred on me? I will take from your hand the
cup of your sufferings and call on your name. I vow before you
eternal Father and the Holy Spirit, before your most holy Mother
and her most chaste spouse, before the angels, apostles and martyrs,
before my blessed fathers, Saint Ignatius, and Saint Francis Xavier—
in trust I vow to you, Jesus my Savior, that as far as I have the
strength I will never fail to accept the grace of martyrdom, if some
day you in your infinite mercy shall offer it to me, your most unworthy servant.

For this reason, my beloved Jesus, and because of the surging joy
which moves me, here and now I offer my blood and body and life.
May I die only for you, if you will grant me this grace, since you
willingly died for me. Let me so live that you may grant me the gift
of such a happy death. In this way, my God and Savior, I will take
from your hand the cup of your sufferings and call on your name:
Jesus, Jesus, Jesus!

My God, it grieves me greatly that you are not known, that in the
savage wilderness all have not been converted to you, that sin has not

been driven from it. My God, even if all the brutal tortures which prisoners in this region must endure should fall on me, I offer myself most willingly to them and I alone shall suffer them all.

—*St. John de Brebeuf*

OCTOBER 23
St. John of Capistrano

St. John of Capistrano (1386–1456), a lawyer and politician, underwent a conversion during an imprisonment, and joined the Franciscan Order. He was a most effective preacher and confessor.

Those who are called to the table of the Lord must glow with the brightness that comes from the good example of a praiseworthy and blameless life. They must completely remove from their lives the filth and uncleanness of vice. Their upright lives must make them be the salt of the earth for themselves and for the rest of the human family. The brightness of their wisdom must make them like the light of the world that brings light to others. They must learn from the eminent teacher, Jesus Christ, what he declared not only to his apostles and disciples, but also to all the priests and clerics who were to succeed them, when he said, "You are the salt of the earth. But what if salt goes flat? How can you restore its flavor? Then it is good for nothing but to be thrown out and trampled underfoot."

"You are the light of the world." Now a light does not illumine itself, but instead it diffuses its rays and shines all around upon everything that comes into its view. So it must be with the glowing lives of upright and holy clerics. By the brightness of their holiness they must bring light and serenity to all who gaze upon them. They have been placed here to care for others. Their own lives should be an example to others, showing how they must live in the house of the Lord.

—*St. John*

OCTOBER 24
St. Anthony Claret

St. Anthony Claret (1807–1870) was a weaver who went on to become a parish priest, a missionary, archbishop of Cuba, confessor to the Queen of Spain, and a publisher, ending his life in the solitude of a Cistercian monastery. He founded the Missionary Sons of the Immaculate Heart of Mary, or the Claritians.

The love of Christ arouses us, urges us to run and to fly, lifted on the wings of holy zeal. The zealous man desires and achieves all great things and he labors strenuously so that God may always be better known, loved and served in this world and in the life to come, for this holy love is without end.

Because he is concerned also for his neighbor, the man of zeal works to fulfill his desire that all be content on this earth and happy and blessed in their heavenly homeland, that all may be saved, and that no one may perish forever, or offend God or remain even for a moment in sin. Such are the concerns we observe in the holy apostles and in all who are driven by the apostolic spirit.

For myself, I say this to you: The one who burns with the fire of divine love is a child of the Immaculate Heart of Mary, and wherever he goes, he enkindles that flame. He desires and works with all his strength to inflame all with the fire of God's love. Nothing deters him. He rejoices in poverty. He labors strenuously. He welcomes hardships. He laughs off false accusation. He rejoices in anguish. He

thinks only of how he might follow Jesus Christ and imitate him by
his prayers, his labors, his sufferings, and by caring always and only
for the glory of God and the salvation of souls.

—St. Anthony

NOVEMBER

NOVEMBER 1
All Saints

Today we honor all in heaven, both the known and the unknown, all who have accepted the saving grace of Christ, explicitly or implicitly.

Why should our praise and glorification, or even the celebration of this feast mean anything to the saints? What do they care about earthly honors when their heavenly Father honors them by fulfilling the faithful promise of the Son? The saints have no need of honor from us; neither does our devotion add the slightest thing to what is theirs. Clearly, if we venerate their memory it serves us, not them. But I tell you, when I think of them, I feel inflamed by tremendous yearning.

Calling the saints to mind arouses in us, above all else, a longing to enjoy their company, so desirable in itself. In short, we long to be united in happiness with all the saints. But our dispositions change. The Church of all the first followers of Christ awaits us, but we do nothing about it. The saints want us to be with them, and we are indifferent. The souls of the just await us, and we ignore them.

Come, brothers, let us at length spur ourselves on. We must rise again with Christ, we must seek the world which is above and set our mind on the things of heaven. Let us long for those who are longing for us, hasten to those who are waiting for us, and ask those who look for our coming to intercede for us. We should not only want to be with the saints, we should also hope to possess their happiness. While we desire to be in their company, we must also earnestly seek to share in their glory. Do not imagine there is anything harmful in such an ambition as this; there is no danger in setting our hearts on such glory.

Therefore we should aim at attaining this glory with a whole-hearted and prudent desire. That we may rightly hope and strive for such blessedness, we must above all seek the prayers of the saints. Thus, what is beyond our own powers to obtain will be granted through their intercession.

—St. Bernard of Clairvaux

NOVEMBER 2
All Souls

The Church sets apart a day for special remembrance of those who have gone before us but have not yet attained the glory of the saints.

By the merits of his bitter passion joined to mine and far surpassing in merit for me all that I can suffer myself, his bounteous goodness shall release me from the pains of purgatory and shall increase my rewards in heaven besides.

—St. Thomas More

NOVEMBER 4
St. Charles Borromeo

St. Charles Borromeo (1538–1584), an outstanding canon lawyer, was named cardinal archbishop of Milan. He did much to promote the reforms of the Council of Trent with great pastoral solicitude and compassion.

I admit that we are all weak, but if we want help, the Lord God has given us the means to find it easily. Would you like me to teach you how to grow from virtue to virtue and how, if you are already recollected at prayer, you can be even more attentive next time and so give God more pleasing worship? Listen, and I will tell you. If a tiny spark of God's love already burns within you, do not expose it to the wind, for it may get blown out. Keep the stove tightly shut so that it will not lose its heat and grow cold. In other words, avoid distractions as well as you can. Stay quiet with God. Do not spend your time in useless chatter.

If teaching and preaching is your job, then study diligently and apply yourself to whatever is necessary for doing your job well. Be sure that you first preach by the way you live. If you do not, your words will bring only cynical laughter and a derisive shake of the head.

We must meditate before, during and after everything we do. The prophet says, "I will pray, and then I will understand." This is the way we can easily overcome the countless difficulties we have to face day after day, which, after all, are part of our work. In meditation we find the strength to bring Christ to birth in ourselves and in others.

—St. Charles

NOVEMBER 9
St. Elizabeth of the Trinity

St. Elizabeth of the Trinity (1880–1906), even before she entered the Carmel of Dijon at twenty-one, had a profound sense of the indwelling Trinity. She rapidly attained great holiness, dying only five years after she entered.

"If you knew the gift of God," Christ said to the Samaritan woman. Yet what is this gift of God but himself? "He came to his own home, and his own people received him not," declared the Beloved Disciple. To many a soul might Saint John Baptist utter the reproach: "Among you stands one whom you do not know." "If you knew the gift of God!"

There is one created being who did know that gift of God, who lost no particle of it; a creature so pure and luminous that she seemed to be the Light itself: Mirror of Righteousness—a being whose life was so simple, so lost in God, that there is but little to say of it: the faithful Virgin, who "kept all these things in her heart." She was so lowly, so hidden in God, in the seclusion of the temple, that she drew upon herself the regard of the Holy Trinity: "Because he has regarded the humility of his handmaid, for behold from henceforth all generations shall call me blessed." The Father, bending down to this lovely creature, so unaware of her own beauty, chose her for the Mother in time of him whose Father he is in eternity. Then the Spirit of Love, who presides over the works of God, overshadowed her; the Virgin uttered her *Fiat:* "Behold the handmaid of the Lord; be it done to me according to your word" and the greatest of all mysteries was accomplished. By the descent of the Word into her womb, Mary became God's own for ever and ever.

—St. Elizabeth

NOVEMBER 10
St. Leo the Great

St. Leo the Great (d. 461) was elected Pope in 440 and fathered the city during the last days of the Roman empire. He has left us many rich and fruitful homilies.

Every believer, no matter where he may be living in the world, when he is regenerated breaks away from his old origin and becomes a new person. Henceforth he is no longer a member of the lineage of his parents according to the flesh, but of the Savior's who made himself man that we might become sons and daughters of God. For had he not come down to us through humility, no one of us could have attained to him through our own merits.

—*St. Leo*

NOVEMBER 11
St. Theodore the Studite

St. Theodore the Studite (759–826) established a monastic community in Constantinople at the Studium, which grew to over a thousand monks, and left rich monastic teaching. He died in exile because of his opposition to the iconoclasts.

Never has anyone been nearer to God than the blessed and most wonderful Virgin Mary. Who could be purer? who more sinless? She was loved so ardently by God, the divine, infinitely pure light, that he made himself one in substance with her through the power of the Holy Spirit and was born of her as perfect man, while keeping entire his own unchangeable and unblended nature. How marvelous this is! In his immense love for us, God was not ashamed to take for his mother her who was his handmaid. What condescension! In his infinite goodness he did not hesitate to become a child of her whom he himself had made. He was truly in love with the most gracious of his creatures and he took her who was of greater worth than the heavenly powers.

Rejoice, House of God, land on which God has stepped, you who have contained in your body him whose divinity overflows all bounds. From you he who is simplicity itself has taken our complex nature; the Eternal has entered into time and the Infinite into limits. Rejoice, House of God, resplendent with the light of divinity. Rejoice, Full of Grace, your deed and your name are more joy-giving than all joy. From you immortal joy, Christ, has come into the world, the cure for the sadness of us all. Rejoice, paradise happier than the garden of Eden, where all virtue has grown and where the tree of life has flourished.

—*St. Theodore*

NOVEMBER 15
St. Albert the Great

St. Albert the Great (1206–1280), one of the leading scientists of his time, on entering the Dominican Order became an excellent theologian and taught Thomas Aquinas. He served for a time as bishop of Regensburg.

"Do this in remembrance of me." Two things should be noted here. The first is, the command that we should use this sacrament, which is indicated when Jesus says, "Do this." The second is that this sacrament commemorates the Lord's going to death for our sake.

The sacrament is profitable because it grants remission of sins; it is most useful because it bestows the fullness of grace on us in this life. "The Father of Spirits instructs us in what is useful for our sanctification." And his sanctification is in Christ's sacrifice, that is, when he offers himself in this sacrament to the Father for our redemption, to us for our use.

Christ could not have commanded anything more beneficial, for this sacrament is the fruit of the tree of life. Anyone who receives this sacrament with the devotion of sincere faith, will never taste death. "It is a tree of life for those who grasp it, and blessed is he who holds it fast. The one who feeds on me shall live on account of me."

—St. Albert

NOVEMBER 16
St. Gertrude

*In St. Gertrude (1256–1301), nature and grace united in an extraor-
dinary degree. She was a highly learned woman and also blessed
with many visions of the Lord. She left a rich literary heritage.*

I salute you through the Sacred Heart of Jesus, all you holy angels
and saints of God; I rejoice in your glory and I give thanks to the
Lord for all the benefits which he has showered on you. I praise him
and glorify him and offer you, for an increase of your joy and honor,
the most gentle heart of Jesus. Deign, therefore, to pray for me so
that I may become holy according to the heart of God.

—*St. Gertrude*

NOVEMBER 17
St. Gregory Thaumaturgus

St. Gregory Thaumaturgus (c. 213–268), the "wonder worker," was converted to Christianity by Origen, later elected bishop of Neacaesarea in Asia Minor. He received the first recorded vision of the Blessed Virgin.

There is one God, the Father of the living Word, who is his subsistent Wisdom and Power and eternal image, perfect begetter of the perfect begotten, Father of the only-begotten Son.

There is one Lord, Only of the Only, God of God, Image and Likeness of Deity, efficient Word, Wisdom comprehensive of the constitution of all things, and Power formative of the whole creation, true Son of true Father, Invisible of Invisible, and Incorruptible of Incorruptible, and Immortal of Immortal, and Eternal of Eternal.

And there is one Holy Spirit, having his subsistence from God and being made manifest to us by the Son, Perfect Image of the Perfect, Life, the Cause of Living, Holy Font, Sanctity.

—St. Gregory

NOVEMBER 18
Dedication of the Basilicas of St. Peter and St. Paul

The basilica of St. Peter on the Vatican Hill and that of St. Paul on the Ostian Way were first constructed in the fourth century. They are two of the four major basilicas of Rome, whose anniversaries the entire Western Church celebrates.

Today, my brethren, we celebrate a great festival. It is very easy for me to say that, but if you ask me what saint's festival it is that we are keeping, it will not perhaps be so easy to answer. Each time that we celebrate the memory of an apostle, or of a martyr or of a confessor, there is no difficulty in indicating with whom we are concerned. Now, today's solemnity is not about any one of them, and yet it is a solemnity and not one of the least. If you want to know, it is the festival of the house of the Lord, of the temple of God, of the city of the eternal King, of the Bride of Christ.

Let us now ask ourselves what in the world can be the house of God, his temple, his city, his Bride. I can only tell you, with awe and reverence: it is we ourselves. Yes, indeed, it is we who are all that, but in the heart of God. We are all that through his grace and not through our own merits. We must be careful not to usurp the property of God and to derive glory from it for ourselves, or God, who made us what we are, will if we exalt ourselves, cast us down.

Childish fervor impels us to try to save ourselves without him, that is precisely what will not happen. If we conceal distress we exclude ourselves from loving kindness, and when we take merit for granted there is no longer any room for grace. On the contrary, the humble admission of our affliction calls forth compassion. It is only because of this admission that God is ready himself to provide for us in our hunger, like a wealthy head of a family, and to enable us to find close to him bread in abundance. And so, we are indeed his house, where the food of life is never lacking.

Therefore, my brethren, since we have proof we are the house of the Father of the family because of the abundance of the food that he provides, the temple of God because of our life in communion, the bride of the immortal Bridegroom because of love, it seems to me that I can declare without fear: this festival is indeed our own.

—St. Bernard of Clairvaux

NOVEMBER 21
Presentation of Mary

Tradition honors the lifetime dedication of Mary to doing the will of God by commemorating her presentation into the Temple at an early age.

Daily, daily sing to Mary,
Sing, my soul, her praises due;
All her feasts, her actions worship,
With the heart's devotion true.

Lost in wondering contemplation
Be her majesty confessed.
Call her Mother, call her Virgin,
Happy Mother, Virgin blest.

—St. Bernard of Cluny

NOVEMBER 23
St. Clement of Rome

St. Clement of Rome (d. 99), a Roman converted by St. Peter, became Pope in 91, suffered exile, and died for the faith.

We will ask, with instancy of prayer and supplication, that the Creator of the Universe may keep intact to the end the number that has been numbered of his elect throughout the world through his beloved Son Jesus Christ, through whom he called us out of darkness into light, from ignorance to the full knowledge of the glory of his name.

Grant to us, Lord, that we may set our hope on your name which is the primal source of all creation. Open the eyes of our heart that we may know you, who alone are highest in the high, holy in the holy, who lay low the insolence of the proud, who scatter the imagination of the nations, who set the lowly on high and bring the lofty low, who make the rich and make the poor, who kill and make alive, who alone is the Benefactor of spirits and the God of all flesh, who look into the abyss, who scan our works, the Succor of those in peril, the Savior of those in despair, the Creator and Overseer of every spirit, who multiply the nations on earth and choose out from all those who love you through Jesus Christ, your beloved Son, through whom you did instruct us, sanctify us, honor us. We beseech you, Lord and Master, be our help and succor, save those among us who are in tribulations, have mercy on the lowly, lift up the fallen, show yourself to the needy, heal the ungodly, convert the wanderers of your people, feed the hungry, release our prisoners, raise up the weak, comfort the fainthearted, let all nations know that you are God, you alone, with Jesus Christ, your Son, and we are your people, the sheep of your pasture.

—St. Clement

NOVEMBER 24
St. Columban

St. Columban (c. 540–615), a great Irish missionary monk, estab-
lished monasteries in many parts of Europe and left a monastic rule
widely observed in the course of the next two centuries.

Moses wrote in the Law, "God made us in his image and after his
likeness." Consider, I beg you, the importance of this word. God, the
all-powerful, the invisible, the incomprehensible, the inestimable, in
fashioning us out of clay, ennobled us with the image of his own
grandeur. What is there in common between us and God, between
clay and spirit? For "God is spirit." It is therefore a great mark of
esteem for us that God should have bestowed upon us the image of
his eternity and the likeness of his own life. Our grandeur is in our
likeness to God, provided that we retain it. . . .

As long as we make good use of the virtues which are planted in
us, we will be like God. God has taught us that we shall have to give
back to him all the virtues which he has put in us from the moment
of our creation. He asks us in the first place to love God with all our
heart, because "he first loved us," from the very beginning, even
before we existed. To love God, therefore, is to renew his image in
ourselves. Now, it is the person who keeps God's commandments
who loves God. God said in effect, "If you love me, you will keep my
commandments." His commandment is mutual love, according to
this word, "A new commandment I give to you, that you love one
another, even as I have loved you." And true love consists "not in
word or speech," but "in deed and truth." It is for us, then, to reflect
for our God, for our Father, the inviolate image of his holiness, for
he is holy, and he said: "Be holy, for I am holy," with love, for he is

love—John said, "God is love."—with tenderness and in truth, for God is good and true.

Do not let us be painters of a strange image. In order not to introduce into ourselves the image of pride, let us allow Christ to paint his image in us.

—*St. Columban*

NOVEMBER 30
St. Andrew

St. Andrew (first century), apostle of the Lord, brother of St. Peter, traditionally died on a cross for Christ.

O great Saint Andrew, your name, a token of beauty, foretells your splendor in the glory of your holy cross. The cross exalts you, the blessed cross loves you, the bitter cross prepares the joys of light to come for you.

The mystery of the cross shines in you with a twofold beauty: for by the cross you vanquished insults and taught all of the Divine Blood shed on the cross. Give fervor to our languid hearts and take us under your care, that by the victory of the cross we may reach our home in heaven. Amen.

—*Pope St. Damasus I*

DECEMBER

DECEMBER 3
St. Francis Xavier

St. Francis Xavier (1506–1552), a well-educated, noble Basque, was one of the first Jesuits to make profession and to go forth on mission. He was called "Apostle of India," and his exploits rivaled if not surpassed those of St. Paul himself.

I have now entered on the third year since my departure from Lisbon. . . . How many conversions to Christianity still remain to be effected in the countries in which I find myself, simply for lack of people who are concerned with such godly and holy things. How often I am seized with a desire to go to the universities of Europe, shouting at the top of my voice, like a man who is out of his mind, and especially to the University of Paris, right in the midst of the Sorbonne, to tell those who have more knowledge than desire, to put it to good use. How many souls are led astray from the path of glory and go to hell simply because of their indifference. If in the same way that they seek to acquire learning they would seek to discover the account which our Lord God will ask of them and the talent which he has given them, many of them would be roused. They would employ such means and spiritual exercises as would enable them to know and penetrate in the depths of their souls, the divine will, and they would conform more closely to it than to their own inclinations, saying, "Lord, here I am, what would you have me to do? Send me where you will; and if it seem good to you, even to the Indians." How much more happily would they live and with the great hope of obtaining the divine mercy at the hour of their death, when they will present themselves for individual judgment which no man can escape, for they would be able to plead in their favor, "Lord, you gave me five talents, here are another five which I have gained."

I was on the point of writing to the University of Paris, or at least to our Master de Cornibus and to Doctor Picardo to tell them of the thousands and millions of heathen who would become Christian if there were workers in the field. So great is the multitude of those who are being converted to faith in Christ in this country in which I find myself that often my arms are exhausted with baptizing people. In the same way I can sometimes scarcely speak after having repeated so often the Creed and the commandments in their language, together with the prayers and some teaching which I have prepared in which I explain to them what it means to be a Christian, what we mean by paradise and hell and who goes to the one or the other. Most often I repeat the Creed and the commandments. Some days I baptize a whole village.

—St. Francis Xavier

DECEMBER 4
St. John Damascene

St. John Damascene (c. 675–c. 749), born in Damascus, served under the caliph prior to entering the monastery of St. Saba, outside of Jerusalem. He became one of the greatest theological writers of the Eastern Christianity and was declared a Doctor of the Church.

And you, O Church, are a most excellent assembly, the noble summit of perfect integrity, whose assistance comes from God. You, devout Christians, receive from us a statement of the Father that is free from error, to strengthen the Church, just as our fathers handed it down to us.

—St. John

DECEMBER 7
St. Ambrose of Milan

*St. Ambrose of Milan (c. 340–397), a powerful Roman official, was
elected bishop of Milan prior to his baptism. This Doctor of the
Church, by his preaching and teaching, including the conversion of
St. Augustine, did much to consolidate Christianity in the West.*

All who are led by the Spirit are children of God. They are children
of God insofar as they do not receive a spirit of slavery, but the spirit
of the children of adoption, so that the Holy Spirit bears witness with
our spirit that we are children of God. The witness of the Holy Spirit
consists in this: that he is sent into our heart, crying, "Abba, Father!"
as the Apostle wrote to the Galatians. But there is another great
witness to our divine adoption: it is that we are heirs of God and
fellow heirs with Christ. They are fellow heirs with Christ who are
glorified with him. They are glorified with Christ who suffer with
him and have shared his passion. And to encourage us to suffer with
him, Saint Paul adds that all our sufferings are not worth comparing
with the great blessings which will be granted us in reward for our
pains, and which will be manifest in us when, recreated in the image
of God, we are given the grace to behold this glory face to face.

—*St. Ambrose*

DECEMBER 8
Feast of the
Immaculate Conception

In 1854 Pope Pius IX solemnly proclaimed the common belief of Christians that the Blessed Virgin Mary through the foreseen merits of her Son was preserved free from contracting original sin and was at her conception full of grace.

All men sinned in Adam (Rom. 5:12). This statement is certainly true and I declare it would be impious to deny it. But when I consider the eminence of God's grace in you, Mary, I find that in a truly remarkable way you were placed not among but above all other creatures; hence I conclude that in your conception you were not bound by the law of nature like others, but by the extraordinary power and operation of divinity, in a way transcending human reason, you were preserved from all taint of sin.

—St. Eadmer of Canterbury

DECEMBER 12
Our Lady of Guadalupe

In December 1531, less than forty years after the discovery of the New World, the Blessed Virgin Mary appeared to a Mexican Indian and left a picture of herself on his cloak as a sign of her maternal care.

I vividly desire that a church be built on this site, so that in it I can be present and give my love, compassion, help, and defense, for I am your most devoted mother . . . to hear your laments and to remedy all your miseries, pains, and sufferings.

—*Our Lady of Guadalupe*

DECEMBER 14
St. John of the Cross

*St. John of the Cross (1542–1591), the author of spiritual classics,
worked for the reform of the Carmelite order. He suffered a great
deal of persecution from Church authorities.*

The more the air is cleansed of vapor and the quieter and purer it is,
the more the sun illumines and warms it. We should not bear attach-
ment to anything, not to the practice of meditation or any consolation, sensory or spiritual, nor to any other insights. We should seek
to be free and detached from all things, because any thought or
discursive reflection or consolation upon which we lean will impede
and disquiet us. It will make noise within the profound silence which
we are given to possess for the sake of a deep and delicate listening.
God speaks to the heart in this inner solitude, which he spoke of in
Hosea. In supreme peace and tranquility, we listen, like David, to
what the Lord God speaks to us for he speaks his peace in this
solitude.

—St. John

DECEMBER 21
St. Peter Canisius

St. Peter Canisius (1521–1597), a Jesuit called the "Second Apostle of Germany," wrote one of the first catechisms.

It was as if you opened to me the heart of your most sacred body. I seemed to see it directly before my eyes. You told me to drink from this fountain, inviting me, that is, to draw the waters of my salvation from your wellsprings, my Savior. I was most eager that streams of faith, hope, and love should flow into me from that source. I was thirsting for poverty, chastity, obedience. I asked to be made wholly clean by you, to be clothed by you, to be made resplendent by you.

So, after daring to approach your most loving heart and to plunge my thirst in it, I received a promise from you of a garment made of three parts: these were to cover my soul in its nakedness, and to belong especially to my religious profession. They were peace, love, and perseverance. Protected by this garment of salvation, I was confident that I would lack nothing but all would succeed and give you glory.

—*St. Peter*

DECEMBER 25
The Nativity of Our Lord and Savior Jesus Christ

Dearly Beloved, today our Savior is born; let us rejoice. Sadness should have no place on the birthday of life. The fear of death has been swallowed up; life brings us joy with the promise of eternal happiness.

No one is shut out from this joy; all share the same reason for rejoicing. Our Lord, victor over sin and death, finding no one free from sin, came to free us all.

In the fullness of time, chosen in the unfathomable depths of God's wisdom, the Son of God took for himself our common humanity in order to reconcile it with its creator. He came to overthrow the devil, the origin of death, in that very nature by which the devil had overthrown the human family.

Let us throw off our old nature and all its ways and, as we have come to birth in Christ, let us renounce the works of the flesh.

Christian, remember your dignity, and now that you share in God's own nature, do not return by sin to your former base condition. Bear in mind who is your head and of whose body you are a member. Do not forget that you have been rescued from the power of darkness and brought into the light of God's kingdom. Through baptism you have become a temple of the Holy Spirit.

—St. Leo the Great

DECEMBER 26
St. Stephen

Saint Stephen, one of the first seven deacons, was the first to shed his blood for the Risen and Glorious Christ, as is recounted in the Acts of the Apostles.

Yesterday we celebrated the birth in time of our eternal king. Today, we celebrate the triumphant suffering of his soldier. Yesterday our King, clothed in his robe of flesh, left his place in the virgin's womb and graciously visited the world. Today, his soldier leaves the tabernacle of his own body and goes triumphantly to heaven.

The love that brought Christ from heaven to earth raised Stephen from earth to heaven; shown first in the King, it later shone forth in his soldier. His love for his neighbor made him pray for those who were stoning him. Love inspired him to reprove those who erred, to make them amend; love led him to pray for those who stoned him to save them from punishment.

Love, indeed, is the source of all good things. It is an impregnable defense, and the way that leads to heaven. He who walks in love can neither go astray nor be afraid. Love guides him, protects him and brings him to the journey's end.

—*St. Fulgentius of Ruspe*

DECEMBER 27
St. John

St. John, the disciple whom Jesus loved, received the care of Mary at the cross. Traditionally he went to minister at Ephesus and was exiled on Patmos, the only one of the Twelve not to die a martyr's death.

Something that has existed since the beginning, that we have heard, and we have seen with our own eyes; that we have watched and touched with our hands: the Word, who is life—this is our subject. That life was made visible: we saw it and we are giving our testimony, telling you of the eternal life which was with the Father and has been made visible to us. What we have seen and heard we are telling you so that you, too, may be in union with us, as we are in union with the Father and with his Son Jesus Christ. We are writing this to you to make your own joy complete.

This is what we have heard from him and the message that we are announcing to you: God is light; there is no darkness in him at all.

—St. John

DECEMBER 28
The Holy Innocents

St. Matthew recounts how King Herod ordered the slaughter of all the little boys in Bethlehem in an effort to kill the Messiah. The Church has honored these little ones as martyrs, dying for Christ's sake.

Why are you afraid, Herod, when you hear of the birth of a king? He does not come to drive you out, but to conquer the devil. But because you do not understand this you are disturbed and in a rage. To destroy one child whom you seek, you show your cruelty in the death of so many children.

You are not restrained by the love of weeping mothers or fathers mourning the deaths of their sons, not by the cries and sobs of the children. You destroy those who are tiny in body because fear is destroying your heart. You imagine that if you accomplish your desire you can prolong your own life, though you are seeking to kill Life himself.

The children die for Christ, though they do not know it. The parents mourn for the death of martyrs. The Christ child makes of those as yet unable to speak fit witnesses to himself. But you, Herod, do not know this and are disturbed and furious. While you vent your fury against the child, you are already paying him homage, and do not know it.

—St. Quodvultdeus

DECEMBER 29
St. Thomas Becket

St. Thomas Becket (1118–1170), a friend of Henry II of England, served him as chancellor before becoming archbishop of Canterbury. He suffered exile and then martyrdom for protecting the rights of the Church.

The Roman Church remains the head of all churches and the source of Catholic teaching. Of this there can be no doubt. Everyone knows that the keys of the kingdom of heaven were given to Peter.

Upon his faith and teaching the whole fabric of the Church will continue to be built until we all reach the full maturity in Christ and attain to unity in faith and knowledge of the Son of God.

All important questions that arise among God's people are referred to the judgment of Peter in the person of the Roman Pontiff.

—St. Thomas

DECEMBER 31
The Holy Name of Jesus

The Holy Name of Jesus, the name above all names, has always had a special place in Christian piety.

Jesus is to me honey in the mouth, music in the ear, a song in the heart.

Does one of us feel sad? Let the name of Jesus come into his heart, from there let it spring to his mouth, so that shining like the dawn it may dispel all darkness and make a cloudless sky. Does someone fall into sin? Does his despair even urge him to suicide? Let him but invoke this life-giving name and his will to live will be at once renewed. The hardness of heart that is our common experience, the apathy bred of indolence, bitterness of mind, repugnance for the things of the spirit—have they ever failed to yield in presence of that saving name? The tears dammed up by the barrier of our pride—how have they not burst forth again with sweeter abundance at the thought of Jesus' name? And where is the one who, terrified and trembling before impending peril, has not been suddenly filled with courage and rid of fear by calling on the strength of the name? Where is the one who, tossed on the rolling seas of doubt, did not quickly find certitude by recourse to the clarity of Jesus' name? Was ever a man so discouraged, so beaten down by afflictions, to whom the sound of this name did not bring new resolve? In short, for all the ills and disorders to which flesh is heir this name is medicine. For proof we have no less than his own promise: "Call upon me in the day of trouble; I will deliver you, and you shall glorify me." Nothing so curbs the onset of anger, so allays the upsurge of pride. It cures the wound of envy, controls unbridled extravagance and quenches the flame of lust; it cools the thirst of covetousness and banishes the itch of unclean desire. For when I name Jesus I set before me a man who is meek and humble of heart, kind, prudent, chaste, merciful, flawlessly upright and holy in the eyes of all; and this same man is the all-powerful God whose way of life heals me, whose support is my strength. All these re-echo for me at the hearing of Jesus' name.

—*St. Bernard of Clairvaux*

SELECT
BIBLIOGRAPHY

THE SAINTS . . .

In addition to the ancient, colorful hagiographies, many saints are blessed today with interesting, well-written, and well-documented biographies. Besides the general sources, such as *New Catholic Encyclopedia* and such classics as Butler's *Lives of the Saints* (which was recently reprinted), there are a number of collective biographical studies available. We indicate here only a few that can be easily obtained for home use.

Saints and Feast Days (Loyola University Press, Chicago, 1986).

Delaney, John J., *Pocket Dictionary of Saints* (Doubleday & Company, Inc., Garden City, N.Y., 1983).

Dooley, Kate, *The Saints Book* (Paulist Press, Mahwah, N.J., 1981).

Foley, Leonard, O.F.M., ed., *Saint of the Day,* 2 vols. (Saint Anthony Messenger Press, Cincinnati, 1981).

Hoagland, Victor, C.P., *The Book of Saints* (Regina Press, New York, 1986).

McBride, Alfred, *Saints Are People* (Wm. C. Brown Company Publishers, Dubuque, Iowa, 1981).

Tylenda, Joseph N., S.J., *Jesuit Saints and Martyrs* (Loyola University Press, Chicago, 1984).

. . . AND THEIR WRITINGS

Again, our times are blessed with many new translations and editions of the writings of the saints. Besides individual volumes, many fine collections are in production at the present time.

Ancient Christian Writers (Paulist Press, Mahwah, N.J.) offers the early Christian Fathers.

Fathers of the Church (The Catholic University of America Press, Washington, D.C.) offers a more extensive collection of the same.

Cistercian Fathers (Cistercian Publications, Kalamazoo, Mich.) presents the writings of the early Cistercian Fathers, Bernard of Clairvaux, Aelred of Rievaulx, etc.

Cistercian Studies (Cistercian Publications, Kalamazoo, Mich.) presents the writings of many monastic saints through the centuries.

Classics of Western Spirituality (Paulist Press, Mahwah, N.J.) includes works from other traditions along with a wide selection of Christian authors.

ABOUT THE AUTHOR

Father M. Basil Pennington, o.c.s.o. is a Cistercian (Trappist) monk of Assumption Abbey, Ava, Missouri. He entered the Abby of Our Lady of Saint Joseph in Spencer, Massachusetts, in 1951 after graduating from Cathedral College, Brooklyn, N.Y. After ordination in 1956 he spent several years in Rome gaining an S.T.L. *cum laude* from the Pontifical University of Saint Thomas Aquinas and a J.C.L. *summa cum laude* from the Gregorianum. He assisted at the Second Vatican Council as a peritus and in the preparation of the new Code of Canon Law. With Thomas Merton he started Cistercian Publications in 1968 and founded the Institute of Cistercian Studies at Western Michigan University in 1973. Father became nationally known through his efforts to help the American Church refind its contemplative dimension through the Centering Prayer movement. For four years he served as a vocational father in his Order, lecturing widely and publishing a book on vocational discernment. Father has published over twenty books and some 400 articles in various languages. His most recent publications are *Mary Today,* published at the opening of the Marian Year, a personal study of Thomas Merton; and book on spirituality for priests.

OTHER IMAGE BOOKS

OTHER IMAGE BOOKS

OTHER IMAGE BOOKS

A 87-3